George Hugg

Sunlight in sacred song

New collection of gems for the Sunday school

George Hugg

Sunlight in sacred song
New collection of gems for the Sunday school

ISBN/EAN: 9783337269517

Printed in Europe, USA, Canada, Australia, Japan

Cover: Foto ©Thomas Meinert / pixelio.de

More available books at **www.hansebooks.com**

SUNLIGHT

IN

Sacred Song

BY

GEO. C. HUGG.

New Collection of Gems for the Sunday School.

VICTORY!

Processional.

Arr. by Geo. C. Hugg.   Arr. by Geo. C. Hugg.

CHORUS.

We march, we march to vic - to - ry ! With the cross of the Lord be--

fore us, With His lov - ing Eye look-ing down from the sky, And His

Ho - ly Arm spread o'er us.

1. We come in the might of the
2. We tread to the roll of the
3. Then on - ward we march our

Lord of light, With meas - ured tread to meet Him; And we
or - gan swell, With watchword du - ly giv - en; And we
arms to prove, With Christ's own flag be - fore us; With His

(2)

VICTORY! Concluded.

put to flight the ar-mies of night, That the sons of the day might greet Him.
urge the Prince of the hosts of hell, To fight for the gates of Heav - en.
Eye of love looking down from above, And His ho-ly Arm spread o'er us.

CHORUS.

We march, we march to vic - to - ry! With the

cross of the Lord be - fore us, With His lov - ing Eye look-ing

down from the sky, And His ho - ly Arm spread o'er us.

HE AROSE.

Geo. C. Hugg.
Geo. C. Hugg.

Slowly.

1. Low - ly entombed He lay, My bless - ed Sav - iour;
2. Vain - ly they watch Him, now, My bless - ed Sav - iour;
3. Burst - ing the seal, He rose, My bless - ed Sav - iour;

Wait - ing the prom - ised day, My prec - ious Lord.
Sure - ly He'll keep His vow, My prec - ious Lord.
Scatter - ing His arm - ed foes, My prec - ious Lord.

Chorus. *faster.*

Up from the tomb He a-rose! And in triumph, vanquish'd all His
He a-rose!

foes, . . He a-rose a victor o'er the realms of night ; And He reigns forever with His
all His foes,

saints in light, He a-rose, He a - rose, Victor o-ver all His foes.
He arose, He arose,

PRAISE THE LORD.

Henrietta E. Blair.   Wm. J. Kirkpatrick.

1. On the cold bar-ren hills I had wan-dered a-far— I was
2. Oh, the joy that I feel I can nev-er re-veal,There is
3. Praise the Lord, O my soul, for the work He has done,For His

wea-ry as wea-ry could be—When the kind,lov-ing voice of the
light where my path-way was dim; I was lost till He came,now by
good-ness and mer-cy to me, For the hope of a rest, in the

REFRAIN.

Saviour I heard,And I knew He was seek-ing for me. Praise the
faith in His name, I am trust-ing my fu-ture to Him.
land of the blest,Where for-ev-er with Him I shall be.

Lord,praise the Lord,O my soul,rejoice and sing;Praise the Lord for His love to me; He re-

deemed me with His blood,Oh,the precious,cleansing flood,Halle-lu-jah,praise the Lord.

6

SEND THE LIGHT.

C. H. G.

CHAS. H. GABRIEL.

1. There's a call comes ringing o'er the restless wave, "Send the light! Send the
2. We have heard the Ma-ce-do-nian call to-day, "Send the light, Send the
3. Let us pray that grace may everywhere abound, Send the light, Send the
4. Let us not grow wea-ry in the work of love, Send the light, Send the

Send the light!

light!" There are souls to res-cue, there are souls to save, Send the
light!" And a gold-en off'ring at the cross we lay, Send the
light! And a Christ-like spir-it every-where be found, Send the
light! Let us gath-er jew-els for a crown a-bove, Send the

Send the light!

The first eight measures,
CHORUS. (*or Bass Solo,*) *may be omitted.*

light!...... Send the light!...... We will spread the

BASS SOLO.

Send the light! Send the light! We will spread...... the ev-er-

ev-er-lasting light, With a will-ing, willing heart and hand.

-last-ing light With a will-ing heart and hand............ Giving

SEND THE LIGHT. Concluded.

Giv-ing God the glo - ry ev - ermore. We will fol - low

God........ the glo - ry ev - er - more. We will follow His com -

follow His command. Send the light, ... the blessed gos - pel light, Let it

mand. .... Send the light, the blessed gospel light,

shine.........from shore to shore !............ Send the light !...... and let its

Let it shine from shore to shore ! Send the light ! and

ra - diant beams Light the world......... for-ev - er - more.................

let its radiant beams Light the world for-ev - ermore.

RIVER OF LIFE.

HORATIUS BONAR.　　　　　　　　　　　　　　GEO. C. HUGG.

1. Fresh from the throne of glo - ry, Bright in its crys - tal gleam,
2. Stream full of life and glad - ness, Spring of all health and peace,
3. Riv - er of God I greet thee, Not now a - far, but near;

Bursts out the liv - ing foun - tain, Swells on the liv - ing stream.
No harps by thee hang si - lent, Nor hap - py voic - es cease.
My soul to thy still wa - ters Hastes in its thirst-ings here.

CHORUS.

Bless - ed Riv - er, Let me ev - er Feast my eyes on thee;
Tran - quil Riv - er, Let me ev - er Sit and sing by thee;
Ho - ly Riv - er, Let me ev - er Drink of on - ly thee;

Bless - ed Riv - er, Let me ev - er Feast my eyes on thee.
Tran - quil Riv - er, Let me ev - er Sit and sing by thee.
Ho - ly Riv - er, Let me ev - er Drink of on - ly thee.

GOSPEL ARMOUR.

GEO. C. HUGG.
GEO. C. HUGG.

1. "Put on, put on the whole armour of God," And the battle for Je-sus be-
2. "Put on, put on the whole armour of God," Which Apostles of Je-sus once
3. "Put on, put on the whole armour of God," While the thunders of victo-ry

gin; The foe may be strong, and the con-flict be long, But with
wore; They strove in their might, with the co-horts of night, 'Till the
roar; Our crown shines on high, thro' the rift in the sky, Leading

CHORUS.

Je-sus the vict'-ry we'll win. Pressing on............ in gos-pel
laur-els of vict'-ry they bore.
home to the bright E-den shore. pressing on,

arm - our, Soon to win............ the glorious prize, Pressing
armour bright, soon to win, glorious prize,

on............ in gos-pel armour bright, We'll soon win reward in the skies.
Pressing on,

ON TO CONQUEST.

Geo. C. Hugg.   Walter E. Marcy.

Spirited.

1. Clad in the gos - pel arm - our, read - y to go,
2. Clad in the gos - pel arm - our, what news to - day?

An - y-where, ev'rywhere, at my King's command: Clad in the gospel armour
Vic - to - ry! vic - to - ry! thus the couriers say: Clad in the gospel armour

proud - ly I stand, List! 'tis the "Forward march" we'll now meet the foe.
loud - ly they sing, Glo - ry to Je - sus Christ, our lead - er and King.

CHORUS.

On - ward, on to con - quest, un - daunted by the din and
On - ward, on: march-ing on,

ON TO CONQUEST. Concluded.

roar-ing of the bat - tle; March - ing ev - er on - ward we'll
March-ing on, ev - er on,

sing a song of tri-umph o'er and o'er: Glo - ry to Je-sus! let the

war-cry ev - er ring! Glo-ry to Je-sus! He will mighty conquest bring!

Glo - ry be to Je - sus! Sing the ran - som'd throng!

Glo - ry be to Je - sus! is our bat - tle song.

STANDING ON THE ROCK.

Fred Woodrow.

C. C. Case. and C. H. G.

1. Standing on the Rock of A - ges, The Rock of Ages old ; Not shak-en by the
2. Standing on the Rock of A - ges, We view the tranquil soul ; The terrors of the
3. Standing on the Rock of A - ges, No need have we to fear ; God ban-ish-es our

temp - est, Nor bought with beaten gold ; E - ter - nal, firm and sure, A
temp - est, The surg-ing bil-lows roll ; Be trou-bles what they may, And
sor - row, God wipes a - way our tear ; We're watching earn-est - ly, We

refuge strong and free, A-mid the stormy bil - lows Of life's tempestuous sea.
break the waves of care, A-mid the wild commo - tion, We stand in safe-ty there.
trust His promise sure; The crown of great rejoic - ing, For all His saints secure.

Chorus.

Stand - - ing, stand - - ing, Standing on the Rock of A - ges,
Standing on the Rock, I am standing on the Rock,

Stand - - ing, stand - - ing, No need have I to fear.
Standing on the Rock, I am standing on the Rock,

PRAISE YE.

Recessional.

GEO. C. HUGG. GEO. C. HUGG.

With spirit.

Praise ye, Praise ye, Praise ye the Lord!

Praise ye Praise ye, Praise ye the Lord!

Praise ye, Praise ye, Praise ye the Lord!

FINE.

Praise ye, Praise ye, O praise ye the Lord.

PRAISE YE. Continued.

rall.

Mag-ni-fy the Lord Je-ho-vah ev - er, Mag-ni-fy His name for-ev-er

more: Praise ye the Lord! Praise ye the Lord; Hal-le-

* BASS.

PRAISE YE. Concluded.

lu - jah, O praise the Lord ; O mag - ni - fy the Lord Je - ho - vah

ev - er, Mag-ni-fy His name for-ev - er more;

Praise ye the Lord, praise ye the Lord, Hal-le-lu-jah, O praise the Lord.

Wm. H. Keyser & Co., 921 Arch Street, Phila., Pa.

EASTER BELLS!

GEO. C. HUGG.　　　　　　　　　　　　　　　　CIRO PINSUTI.

1. Ring, ring the bells! ring the sweet Easter bells! Gladly the sto - ry tell; Of
2. Ring, ring the bells! ring the sweet Easter bells! Ring notes of joy and love; O
3. Ring, ring the bells! ring the sweet Easter bells! Ring out a gladsome lay; O

Je - sus our Lord who a - rose from the grave, Vic - tor o'er death and hell.
ring out redemption thro' Him who was slain, Yet reigns in Heav'n above.
ring, ring the triumph of Je - sus our King! Who rose this Easter day.

CHORUS.

Ring, ring the bells, let their music swell, Over mountain, o'er vale and glen, 'Till the

earth resound with the magic sound; Of the sweet chiming Easter bells; Of the sweet
[chiming

East-er bells, Then ring the bells; Ring the merry Easter bells.
Ring the bells, the sweet Easter bells;

TRIUMPHANT DAY.

Geo. C. Hugg.   Adam Geibel.

1. With song we cel - e - brate the day, The day that glows with hope and joy;
2. The careless throng esteemed Him not, He bore the scoffs and jeers of men,
3. Then hail! all hail triumphant day, For Christ has conquered man's last foe,

The day when Je-sus rose a - gain, Glad songs of praise our lips employ.
He meekly bowed His head and died, But on this day He rose a- gain.
And death has no do - min-ion now, Ex - al - ted one Thy joy we know.

CHORUS.

Hail! all Hail! triumphant day! We glad-ly sing Thy praise; With heart-felt

thanks and tune-ful lay, We own Thy mighty sway, We own Thy mighty sway.

ONWARD.

Geo. C. Hugg.
CORNET.

John Guest.

Instrument.

1. Lord we come a - gain with songs of glad-ness,
2. For-ward, on - ward like a might-y arm - y

Car - ol - ing Thy praises far and near; .... In our lays we
Moves the Church of God in bright ar - ray, ... March-ing on - ward

ban - ish care and sad - ness, Rais-ing to Thy glorious name our notes of cheer.
on our way to Zi - on, Led by Christ our Risen Lord to end-less day.

CHORUS.

Hal - le - lu - jah! we are press-ing on - ward, Where our Lead - er

ONWARD. Concluded.

bids us forward go, Marching on-ward like a mighty arm-y,

Sa-tan's hosts are fly-ing ev-'ry-where!...... Then for-ward! on-ward!

Christ our ris-en Cap-tain, Leads a-gain His Mighty for-ces far and near.

SONG OF TRIUMPH.

Geo. C. Hugg.

1. Al-le-lu-ia! Sing to Je-sus! His the scep-tre, His the throne;
2. Hark! the songs of Ho-ly Zi-on Thunder like a might-y flood:
3. Al-le-lu-ia! Bread of heav-en, Thou on earth our food our stay;
4. Glo-ry be to God the Fa-ther! Glo-ry be to Christ the Son!

Al-le-lu-ia! His the triumph, His the vic-to-ry a-lone.
"Je-sus out of ev-'ry nation, Hath redeemed us by His blood."
Al-le-lu-ia! Here the sin-ful, Flee to Thee from day to day.
Glo-ry to the Ho-ly Spir-it! One in three, and three in One. A-men.

REDEMPTION'S DAWN.

E. CASWELL.   JOHN GOSS.

1. See, a - mid the winter's snow, Born for us on earth be - low,
2. Lo! with - in a man - ger lies He Who built the star - ry skies;
3. Teach, O teach us, Ho - ly Child, By Thy face so meek and mild,

See, the ten - der Lamb ap - pears, Promised from e - ter - nal years.
He Who, throned in height sublime, Sits a - mid the Cher - u - bim.
Teach us to re - sem - ble Thee In Thy sweet hu - mil - i - ty.

CHORUS.

Hail! Thou ev - er bless-èd Morn, Hail! Redemption's hap - py dawn.

Sing, thro' all Je - ru - sa - lem, Christ is born in Beth - le - hem.

HE HAS COME.

Horatius Bonar.   Adam Geibel.

1. He has come! the Christ of God; Left for us His glad a - bode;
2. He the might - y King has come! Making this poor earth His home,
3. Un - to us a child is born! Ne'er has earth be - held a morn

Stoop-ing from His throne of bliss; To this dark-some wil-der-ness.
Come to bear our sin's sad load; Son of Da - vid, Son of God.
All a - mong the morns of time. Half so glo - rious in its prime.

He, has come! the Prince of peace; Come to bid our sor-rows cease:
He has come, whose name of grace Speaks deliv'rance to our race;
Un - to us a Son is giv'n! He has come from God's own heav'n;

Come to scat-ter, with his light, All the shadows of our night.
Left for us His glad a - bode; Son of Man, and Son of God.
Bring-ing with Him from a - bove, Ho - ly peace and Ho - ly love.

NO SHELTER BUT IN CHRIST.

JAMES L. SMITH.   JNO. R. SWENEY.

1. There is no shel-ter for the soul, On earth, in heaven a-bove,
2. There is no shel-ter from the storm That frowns above our head,
3. There is no ref-uge but in Christ, Tho' we the world should gain,

No shel-ter but in Christ the Lord, No ref-uge but His love.
But in the Lamb of Cal-va-ry Whose blood for all was shed.
The soul with-out His grace is lost, All oth-er hope is vain.

REFRAIN.

Then fly . . . . to the ark where the wea-ry dove Came
Oh, fly,

rit.   *a tempo.*

back to the place of rest, Oh, fly to the arms, . . . to the sheltering
Oh, fly to the arms,   to   the

arms . . . . . Of the Sa-viour that loves thee best,
shel-ter-ing arms.

KING OF LOVE.

Sir Henry W. Baker.
Geo. C. Hugg.

Sprightly.

1. The King of love my Shepherd is, Whose good-ness fail-eth nev - er;
2. Where streams of liv - ing wa - ters flow My ransom'd soul He lead - eth;
3. And so thro' all the length of days, Thy goodness fail-eth nev - er;

I noth-ing lack if . I am His, And He is mine for - ev - er.
And where the verdant pastures grow, With food ce-les - tial feed - eth.
Good Shepherd, may I sing Thy praise Within Thy house for-ev - er.

ADORATION.

John Bowring.
Geo. C. Hugg.

Maestoso.

1. How sweetly flowed the gos - pel's sound From lips of gen - tle - ness and grace,
2. From heav'n He came, of heav'n He spoke, To heav'n He led His foll-'wers' way;
3. "Come, wand'rers ! to my Fa-ther's home, Come, all ye wea - ry ones, and rest;"

When list'ning thousands gath-ered round, And joy and rev-'rence filled the place.
Dark clouds of gloom-y night He broke, Unveil-ing an im - mor-tal day.
Yes, sacred Teacher; we will come, O-bey Thee, love Thee, and be blest.

WE COME ADORING.

GEO. C. HUGG.   DR. JOHN STAINER.

Majestic.

1. Lord of Hosts, we come a-dor-ing; Songs of praise our lips employ,
2. May we en-ter in Thy temple As did saints the promised land;
3. Al - le - lu - ias may we ren-der Thee, O God, in tune-ful lays;

Thro' Thy tem-ple gates ad-vanc-ing, Hymning notes of love and joy.
Thro' the world's di - vid - ed wa-ters, Lead us by Thy guid-ing hand.
For ten thousand ten-der mer-cies, And Thy blessing all our days.

NOTE. Commit words of this charming production of Dr. Stainer to memory if possible, and sing in full glowing style, but not boisterously.

LET THE GLAD BELLS RING.

GEO. C. HUGG.   GEO. C. HUGG.

Joyously.

INTRODUCTION.

LET THE GLAD BELLS RING.—Concluded.

From the old grey tow'r, let the glad bells ring ; While the children's voices in cho-rus sing,

Sweetly praising God in melodious song, For His mercy and love so strong.

Hal-le-lu-jah, we will praise Him, Halle-lu-jah, praise the Lord!

For His blessings without num-ber, For His goodness all our days.

Sweetly ring the bells, with a measured swing, While the children's voices in chorus sing.

NOTE. This chorus was suggested by a beautiful composition by J. L. Hatton, and may be sung over two or three times.

26

CHILDREN, COME.

N. K. Bradford.

Geo. C. Hugg.

1. Jor-dan's wa - ters fair were glid-ing Thro' the meadows sweet,
2. Pe - ter said,"the Mas - ter bear-eth Care and toil al - way,
3. A - ges gone, the child-ren's Sav-iour Still is say - ing "come,"

Where, with ten - der moth-ers guid-ing, Wandered lit - tle feet;
"See the anx - ious look He weareth, Take them hence a - way;"
And in heav'n His lov - ing fa - vor Makes their hap - py home;

Seek-ing Je - sus, they were pressing To the Master's side,
"Let them come, do not de - tain them," Je - sus said so mild,
Room for all, and free - ly giv - en, In that home a - bove,

While His arms in love and bless-ing, Free-ly o - pened wide.
"For of such is God's own kingdom, Pure and un - de - filed."
Room for lit - tle ones in heav - en, Who the Sav - iour love.

CHILDREN, COME.—Concluded.

CHORUS.

Let us seek Him, not de-lay-ing, Strive, and find Him while we may:

For in heav'n He still is say-ing: "Blessed children, come to-day."

THE HEALER.

JAMES MONTGOMERY.   Arr. by GEO. C. HUGG.

Grandly.

1. When like a stran ger on our sphere, Blest Je - sus sojourned here,
2. The eye that roll'd in irksome night, Be-held His face of light;
3. With bounding steps, the halt and lame To their De - liv -'rer came;
4. De - mon - iac mad-ness, dark and wild, In His blest pres-ence smiled;

Where'er He went af - flic-tion fled, The sick took up their bed.
The open-ing ear, the loos-ened tongue, Heard precepts, prais-es sung.
O'er dis-mal tombs He sim - ply said, "Come forth," and raised the dead.
The storm of hor - ror ceased to roll, And rea- son blest the soul.

PASS NOT BY ME.

H. D. GANSE.   WM. B. BLAKE.

1. Lord! I know Thy grace is nigh me, Thee Thy-self I can-not see;
2.   I would see Thee and a-dore Thee, And Thy word the pow'r can give;

Je - sus, Mas-ter! pass not by   me; Son   of   David! pit - y   me.
Hear the sightless soul implore Thee; Let   me   see Thy face and live.

While I   sit   in   wea - ry blindness, Longing   for the blessed light,
Ah! what touch is   this that thrills me? What this burst of strange de-light?

Man - y   taste Thy loving-kind-ness, Lord, I would receive my sight.
Lo!   the rapturous vision fills   me! This   is   Jesus! this is   sight.

HARK! MY SOUL.

F. W. Faber.   Henry Smart.

1. Hark! hark! my soul; An - gel - ic songs are swell - ing
2. On - ward we go, for still we hear them sing - ing,
3. Far, far a - way, like bells at even - ing peal - ing
4. Rest comes at length, though life be long and drear - y,

O'er earth's green fields, and o-cean's wave-beat shore:
"Come, wea - ry souls, for Je - sus bids you come:"
The voice of Je - sus sounds o'er land and sea,
The day must dawn, and darksome night be past:

How sweet the truth those bless - ed strains are tell - ing
And, through the dark its ech - oes sweet - ly ring - ing,
And la - den souls, by thousands meek - ly steal - ing,
Faith's jour-ney ends in wel-come to the wea - ry,

CHORUS.

Of that new life where sin shall be no more. An - gels of Je - sus,
The mus-ic of the Gospel leads us home. An - gels of Je - sus,
Kind Shepherd, turn their weary steps to Thee. An - gels of Je - sus,
And heav'n, the heart's true home, will come at last. An - gels of Je - sus,

An-gels of light, Singing to welcome the pilgrims of the night.

MY ROCK AND FORTRESS.

Psalm XXXI.   Arr. Berthold Tours.

In Thee, O Lord, have I put my trust. . . Let me

nev - er be put to con - fu - - sion. De -

liv - er me . . in Thy right - eous - ness.

Bow down Thine ear to } liv - er me, That Thou may'st save . . me,
me, make haste to de- }

And be Thou my strong rock and house of defense. For Thou art my

MY ROCK AND FORTRESS.—Concluded.

strong rock, my strong rock and my cas - tle. For Thou art my

strong rock, my rock and my cas - tle. For Thou art my strong

rock and cas - - - tle, Be Thou al - so my guide,

be Thou al - so my guide, be Thou al - so my guide,

pp rallentando.   *adagio.*

And lead me, lead me for Thy name's sake.   A - MEN.

pp

WAIT PATIENTLY.

F. R. HAVERGAL.   GEO. C. HUGG.

Moderato.

1. God doth not bid thee wait, To dis-ap-point at last;
2. The wear-y wait-ing times, Are but the muf-fled peals:
3. He doth not bid thee wait, Like drift-wood on the wave,

A gol-den prom-ise fair and great In pre-cept mould is cast,
Low pre-lud-ing ce - les-tial chimes, That hail His char-iot wheels,
For fic-kle chance, or fix-ed fate, To ru-in or to save,

Soon shall the morn-ing gild The dark ho-ri-zon rim,
Trust Him to tune thy voice, To blend with ser-a-phim;
Thine eyes shall sure-ly see, No dist-ant hope or dim,

Thy heart's de-sire shall be ful-filled, Wait pa-tient-ly for Him.
His wait shall is-sue in re-joice, Wait pa-tient-ly for Him.
The Lord thy God a-rose for thee, Wait pa-tient-ly for Him.

ff CHORUS. *Slow.*   *pp*

Wait pa-tient-ly for Him! Wait pa-tient-ly for Him!

HOME.

HORATIUS BONAR.　　　　　　　GEO. C. HUGG.

1. Bathed in un-fad-ing sun-light, It-self a sun-born gem;
2. Calm in her queen ly glo - ry, She sits all joy and light;
3. Walled 'round in cost-ly splen-dor, Streets paved with purest gold;

Fair gleams the glorious cit - y, The new Je - ru - sa - lem.
Pure in her bri - dal beau - ty, Her rai - ment fes - tal white.
Fair home of love and beau - ty! Half ne'er hath yet been told.

CHORUS.

Cit - y fair-est, Splen-dor rar-est, Let me gaze on thee!
Home of glad-ness, Free from sad-ness, Let me dwell in thee!
Home e - ter- nal! Bright and ver-nal! I shall rest in thee!

Cit - y fair-est, Splen-dor rar-est, Let me gaze on thee!
Home of glad-ness, Free from sad-ness, Let me dwell in thee!
Home e - ter- nal! Bright and ver-nal! I shall rest in thee!

SUNLIGHT.

GEO. C. HUGG.   GEO. C. HUGG.

1. In the sunlight, bright and glowing, Rays im-mor-tal 'round me shine,
2. In the sunlight, joy un-bounded; Bliss of bliss, and light of light,
3. In the sunlight, pure, ce - les - tial; Bless-ed sun-light of His love,

Fill'd my soul to o - ver-flow-ing, With the ra - di'n-cy di-vine.
"On the Rock of A - ges founded," Let me climb to Zi-on's height.
Soon we'll pass these scenes terrestrial; Soon we'll reach the heights a-bove.

CHORUS.

In the sunlight, Bless-ed sunlight! Glo-rious sunlight of His love;

In the sunlight, Bless-ed sunlight! Glo-rious sunlight of His love.

NOTHING TO PAY.

F. R. HAVERGAL.
Slowly.

GEO. C. HUGG.

1. Nothing to pay! Ah; nothing to pay! Never a word of ex-cuse to say,
2. Nothing to pay! The debt is so great; What will you do with the awful weight?
3. Nothing to pay! Yes, nothing to pay! Jesus has clear'd all the debt a-way,

Year after year thou hast fill'd the score, Owing the Lord still more and more.
How shall the way of es-cape be made? Nothing to pay, yet all must be paid.
Blotted it out with His bleeding hand! Free and forgiv'n and loved you stand.

CHORUS.
Faster.

Hear......... the voice of Je-sus say, Ver-i-ly thou hast noth-ing to pay!
Hear......... the voice of Je-sus say, Ver-i-ly thou hast noth-ing to pay!
Hear......... the voice of Je-sus say, Ver-i-ly thou hast noth-ing to pay!

Ru-ined now, lost art thou, and yet I for-gave thee all thy debt.
All is charged to my own ac-count, I have paid the full a-mount.
Paid, the debt, and the debt-or's free! Now, I ask thee, "lov'st thou Me?"

SONG OF THE AGES.

Geo. C. Hugg.

Geo. C. Hugg.

With great spirit.

1. Float-ing downward through the midnight, Bursts a glo-rious tide of
2. Shepherds watchful guard are keep-ing, O'er their flocks this star-lit
3. Sweet-ly led to Bethl'hem's man-ger, View-ing there the new-born

song, An-gel voi-ces tuned to sweetness, Roll the migh-ty wave a-
night, Wond'ring at the breaking glo-ry, And the an-gel song so
child, Light of light! and hope of a-ges! God and man, now rec-on-

CHORUS.

long
bright. } "Glory, glo-ry in the highest!" "Peace on earth good-will to men;"
ciled.

Down the a-ges roll the ti-dings, Mortals shout a loud A-men.

TRUSTING.

Tune: Song of the Ages.

1. All my doubts I give to Jesus!
   I've His precious promise heard—
   "I shall never be confounded"—
   I am trusting in His word.

CHORUS.

I am trusting, fully trusting,
  Always trusting in His word.
Yes, I'm trusting, fully trusting,
  Always trusting in His word.

2. All my sin I lay on Jesus!
   He doth wash me in His blood;
   He will keep me pure and holy,
   He will bring me home to God.
                          —CHO.

3. All my fears I give to Jesus!
   Rests my weary soul on Him;
   Tho' my way be hid in darkness,
   Never can His light grow dim.—CHO.

4. All my joys I give to Jesus!
   He is all I want of bliss;
   He of all the worlds is Master—
   He has all I need in this.—CHO.

5. All I am I give to Jesus!
   All my body, all my soul,
   All I have and all I hope for,
   While eternal ages roll.—CHO.

                          J. C. MORGAN.

GLORY TO JESUS.

Tune: Song of the Ages.

1. Glory, glory be to Jesus!
   Glory to His precious name;
   Sweet it is to sound His praises,
   Blest it is to spread His fame.

CHORUS.

Glory, glory, hallelujah!
  Glory be to Jesus' name;
Sweet it is to sound His praises,
  Blest it is to spread His fame.

2. In the place of His rejection,
   Where He suffered, where He died,
   Bursts of holy praise ascending
   Greets the glorious Crucified.—CHO.

3. Here was marred His blessed visage,
   Here His brow was wreathed with thorn,
   Here the object of derision,
   Bitter taunt and mocking scorn.—CHO.

4. Yes, triumphant hallelujahs
   Still arise to greet His name;
   Sweet it is to sound His praises,
   Blest it is to spread His fame.—CHO.

5. On the highest hills of Heaven
   Angels sound aloud His praise;
   Saints on earth send back the greeting,
   Glory be to Jesus' name.—CHO.

                          A VON.

JESUS IS KING.

DR. J. G. HOLLAND.

ADAM GEIBEL.

1. There's a song in the air! There's a star in the sky! There's a
2. There's a tu-mult of joy O'er the won-der-ful birth, For the
3. In the light of that star Lies the a-ges impearled; And that
4. We re-joice in the light, And we ech-o the song That comes

mother's deep pray'r And a baby's low cry! And the star rains its fire while the
Virgin's sweet boy Is the Lord of the earth. Ay! the star rains its fire, and the
song from a-far Has swept over the world. Ev'ry hearth is aflame, and the
down thro' the night From the heavenly throng. Ay! we shout to the lovely e-

Beau-ti-ful sing. For the manger of Beth-lehem cra-dles a King.
Beau-ti-ful sing. For the manger of Beth-lehem cra-dles a King.
Beau-ti-ful sing In the homes of the nations that Je-sus is King.
van-gel they bring, And we greet in His cra-dle our Saviour and King!

CHORUS.

Jesus is King, Jesus is King, For the manger of Bethlehem cradles a King.

SWEET BELLS.

Geo. C. Hugg.　　　　　　　　　　Geo. C. Hugg.

1. List ! the sweetly chiming bells ! Far a-way, far a - way, far a - way;
2. On this ho - ly peaceful night Far a-way, far a - way, far a - way;
3. Bells of Heaven sweetly ring Far a - way, far a - way, far a - way;

Tidings of great joy they bring, Far a-way, far a - way, far a - way.
An - gels sing with pure delight Far a-way, far a - way, far a - way.
Ring in praise of Christ our King Far a-way, far a - way, far a - way.

CHORUS.

Christ is born in Bethlehem, far a-way, Ho-ly an-gels join the strain far away;

Till the vaulted heavens ring, far a - way, far a - way, far a - way.

ALL HAIL!

GEO. C. HUGG.   GEO. C. HUGG.

1. On this bright and glorious morning, Christ the Lord to life a - rose!
2. Vain the watch, the stone all sealéd; "Christ hath burst the gates of Hell!
3. Hail! all hail Thou Mighty Vic-tor! Born to reign, a Prince, and King,

See the seal - ed tomb is o - pen, And with light of promise glows.
Join in song of sweet re-joic - ing And the glo - rious tid-ings tell.
Born, Thy peo - ple to de-liv - er, And safe home to glo-ry bring.

CHORUS.

Hail! all hail! Thou Mighty Vic - tor! Thou hast triumphed o'er Thy foes!

Built in three days, glorious Tem-ple! Life transcends Thy death, and woes.

OVER JORDAN.

Tune: All Hail.

1. Over Jordan! Over Jordan!
   Will the Saviour lead us on.
   Over Jordan! Over Jordan!
   To the land of endless song.

CHORUS.

Over Jordan! Over Jordan!
   Where the Tree of Life doth bloom:
Over Jordan! Over Jordan!
   There's no night! no death! no gloom.

2. Over Jordan! Over Jordan!
   Will the Saviour lead us on.
   Over Jordan! Over Jordan!
   'Midst the bright celestial throng.—CHO

3. Over Jordan! Over Jordan!
   'Cross the sea of glassy wave.
   Over Jordan! Over Jordan!
   Thro' the streets of golden pave.—CHO.

4. Over Jordan! Over Jordan!
   Crowns immortal we shall wear.
   Over Jordan! Over Jordan!
   Life eternal we shall share.—CHO.

5. Over Jordan! Over Jordan!
   Longs my soul to speed away.
   Over Jordan! Over Jordan!
   To the realms of endless day.—CHO.

GEO. C. HUGG.

GOD'S CARE.

Tune: All Hail.

1. God shall charge His angel legions
   Watch and ward o'er thee to keep;
   Tho' thou walk in hostile regions,
   Tho' in desert wilds thou sleep.

CHORUS.

God's protecting wings are o'er thee,
   In His love thou shalt abide:
On His bosom He will bear thee
   Safely thro' whate'er betide.

2. On the lion, vainly roaring,
   On his young thy foot shall tread,
   And, the dragon's den exploring,
   Thou shalt bruise the serpent's head.
                                   —CHO

3. Since with pure and firm affection
   Thou on God hast set thy love,
   'Neath the wings of His protection
   He will shield thee from above.—CHO.

4. Thou shalt call on Him in trouble,
   He will hearken, He will save;
   Here for grief reward thee double,
   Crown with life beyond the grave.
                                   —CHO.

5. God shall charge His angel legions
   Watch and ward o'er thee to keep,
   Tho' thou walk in hostile regions,
   Tho' in desert wilds thou sleep.—CHO.

JAMES MONTGOMERY.

RISEN TO-DAY.

Geo. C. Hugg.   Geo. C. Hugg.

With spirit.

1. See the seal is   rude-ly brok-en! Lo! the stone is rolled a - way!
2. Lo! the tomb is   standing o - pen, And the Ma-rys weep-ing near,
3. Hark! the joyful   tidings ringeth, Christ hath triumphed o'er the grave!

Kept is ev-'ry sign and to-ken; "He is ris-en!" an-gels say.
An-gel tones with-in are spok-en: "He is ris-en, do not fear!"
Joy to all His foll'wers bringeth, Christ hath ris-en!—lives to save!

CHORUS.

"He is ris - en!" "He is ris - en!" See the place where Je-sus lay!

An-gels her - ald the glad tid-ings: Christ, the Lord, a - rose to - day!

HEAVENLY FATHER.

Tune: Risen To-day.

1. Heavenly Father, send Thy blessing
    On Thy children gathered here ;
    May they all, Thy name confessing,
    Be to Thee forever dear.
    Holy Saviour, who in meekness
    Didst vouchsafe a child to be,
    Guide their steps and help their weakness,
    Bless and make them like to Thee.

2. Bear the lambs when they are weary
    In Thine arms and on Thy breast;
    Thro' life's desert, dark and dreary,
    Bring them to Thy heavenly rest.
    Spread Thy wings of blessing o'er them,
    Holy Spirit, from above ;
    Guide, and lead, and go before them,
    Give them peace, and joy; and love.
                            C. WORDSWORTH.

MY KING.

Tune : Risen To-day.

1. God, my King, Thy might confessing,
    Ever will I bless Thy name ;
    Day by day Thy throne addressing,
    Still will I Thy praise proclaim,
    Nor shall fail from memory's treasure
    Works by love and mercy wrought—
    Works of love surpassing measure,
    Works of mercy passing thought.

2. Full of kindness and compassion,
    Slow to anger, vast in love,
    God is good to all creation,
    All His works His goodness prove ;
    All Thy works, O Lord, shall bless Thee,
    Thee shall all Thy saints adore ;
    King supreme shall they confess Thee,
    And proclaim Thy sovereign power.
                            R. MANT.

BEFORE THE CROS

Tune : Risen To-day.

1. Sweet the moments, rich in blessing,
    Which before the Cross we spend ;
    Life, and health, and peace possessing
    From the sinner's dying Friend.
    Fully blessed is this station,
    Low before the Cross to lie ;
    While we see divine compassion
    Beaming in His gracious eye.

2. Here we feel our sins forgiven,
    While upon the Lamb we gaze ;
    And our thoughts are all of heaven,
    And our lips o'erflow with praise.
    Still in ceaseless contemplation
    Fix our hearts and eyes on Thee,
    Till we taste Thy full salvation
    And, unveiled, Thy glories see.
                            J. ALLEN.

COME, THOU FOUNT.

Tune: Risen To-day.

1. Come, thou Fount of every blessing,
    Tune my heart to sing Thy grace;
    Streams of mercy never ceasing,
    Call for songs of loudest praise.
    Teach me some melodious sonnet,
    Sung by flaming tongues above ;
    Praise the mount—I'm fixed upon it!
    Mount of Thy redeeming love.

2. Oh, to grace how great a debtor,
    Daily I'm constrained to be!
    Let Thy goodness, like a fetter,
    Bind my wandering heart to Thee.
    Prone to wander, Lord, I feel it—
    Prone to leave the God I love :
    Here's my heart, oh, take and seal it !
    Seal it for Thy courts above.

ALWAYS WITH US.

E. H. NEVIN.   GEO. C. HUGG.

Joyously.

1. Al-ways with us,   always with us, Words of cheer and words of love;
2. With us when the   storm is sweeping O'er our pathway dark and drear,

Thus the ris - en   Saviour whispers From His dwelling place a - bove,
Wak-ing hope with - in our bosoms, Still-ing ev - ery   anxious fear;

With us when we   toil in   sadness, Sowing much and reaping none,
With us ; in the   lone-ly   val - ley When we cross the chilling stream,

Tell-ing us that   in the fu-ture, Golden harvests   shall be won.
Lighting up the   steps to glo - ry With sal-va-tion 's radiant beam.

O WONDROUS NIGHT.

A. S. DOUGHTY.

GEO. C. HUGG.

Serenely.

1. O won-drous night! when stars se-rene-ly shin-ing,
2. O joy-ous night! when shep-herds heard the sto-ry,
3. O hal-lowed night! when heav'n to earth sent greet-ing.

Il-lumed Ju - de-a's hills, and brightened all the plain;
That an-gel told 'midst light that shone o'er dale and glen;
And heav'n-ly her-ald led the vast se-raph-ic throng;

When bright-er star moved through the heav'ns de-fi-ning
When heav'nly choir, sent from the realms of glo-ry,
May thy glad tidings roll o'er the earth re-peat-ing,

Where Christ, the Prince of Peace, on earth was born to reign.
Sang praise to God on high, Peace and good will to men.
Till the whole world redeemed shall sing re-demption's song.

CHORUS.

O Ho-ly night, Christ the Lord is born.

EASTER LIGHT.

GEO. C. HUGG.
Joyously.

ADAM GEIBEL.

1. The morning light shone faint and dim: With tim - id ea - ger tread,
2. An an - gel mes - sen - ger appears With words of joy - ous cheer;

"The lov - ing Ma - ry's seek the place, Where sleeps their cherished dead;"
The Cru - ci - fied I know ye seek: He's ris'n, He is not here;

The seal - ed stone is rolled a-way, Be-hold the emp - ty tomb!
He lives a - gain, your ris - en Lord, Speed ye with rap - id tread;

They stand and gaze a - while in awe, Oppressed with dread and
And say to His dis - ci - ple band, He lives, He is not

gloom, They stand op - pressed with dread and gloom.
dead! He lives, He lives, He is not dead.

SINNER'S FRIEND.

Tune: Easter Light.

1. Jesus! Thou art the sinner's Friend;
   As such I look to Thee;
   Now, in the fullness of Thy love,
   O Lord! remember me.

2. Thou wondrous Advocate with God!
   I yield myself to Thee;
   While Thou art sitting on Thy throne,
   ||: Dear Lord! :|| remember me.

3. Lord! I am guilty, I am vile,
   But Thy salvation's free;
   Then, in Thine all-abounding grace,
   Dear Lord! remember me.

4. And when I close my eyes in death
   When creature-helps all flee,
   Then, O my dear Redeemer, God!
   ||: I pray, :|| remember me.
   R. BURNHAM.

CROWN HIM.

Tune: Easter Light.

1. All hail the power of Jesus' name!
   Let angels prostrate fall!
   Bring forth the royal diadem,
   And crown Him Lord of all!

2. Ye chosen seed of Israel's race,
   Ye ransomed from the fall,
   Hail Him, who saves you by His grace,
   ||: And crown :|| Him Lord of all!

3. Let every kindred, every tribe,
   On this terrestial ball,
   To Him all majesty ascribe,
   And crown Him Lord of all!

4. Oh, that with yonder sacred throng,
   We at His feet may fall;
   We'll join the everlasting song,
   ||: And crown :|| Him Lord of all!
   E. PERRONET.

FATHER OF MERCIES.

Tune: Easter Light.

1. Father of mercies! in Thy word
   What endless glory shines!
   Forever be Thy name adored
   For these celestial lines.

2. Here the Redeemer's welcome voice
   Spreads heavenly peace around,
   And life and everlasting joys
   ||: Attend :|| the blissful sound.

3. Oh! may these heavenly pages be
   My ever dear delight,

And still new beauties may I see,
And still increasing light.

4. Divine Instructor, gracious Lord!
   Be Thou forever near;
   Teach me to love Thy sacred word,
   ||: And view :|| my Saviour there.
   A. STEELE.

VOICE OF JESUS.

Tune: Easter Light.

1. I heard the voice of Jesus say,
   "Come unto me and rest!
   Lay down, thou weary one, lay down
   Thy head upon my breast."
   I came to Jesus as I was,
   Weary, and worn, and sad;
   I found in Him a resting-place,
   ||: And He :|| has made me glad.

2. I heard the voice of Jesus say,
   "Behold, I freely give
   The living water: thirsty one,
   Stoop down and drink, and live."
   I came to Jesus, and I drank
   Of that life-giving stream;
   My thirst was quenched, my soul revived,
   ||: And now :|| I live in Him.

3. I heard the voice of Jesus say,
   "I am this dark world's light;
   Look unto me: thy morn shall rise
   And all thy days be bright."
   I looked to Jesus, and I found
   In Him my Star, my Sun;
   And in that light of life I'll walk
   ||: Till days :|| of toil are done.
   HORATIUS BONAR.

CHEERFUL SONGS.

Tune: Easter Light.

1. Come, let us join our cheerful songs,
   With angels round the throne;
   Ten thousand thousand are their tongues,
   But all their joys are one.
   "Worthy the Lamb that died," they cry,
   "To be exalted thus!"
   "Worthy the Lamb," our lips reply,
   "For He was slain for us!"

2. Jesus is worthy to receive
   Honor and power divine;
   And blessings, more than we can give,
   Be, Lord! forever thine.
   Let all who dwell above the sky,
   And air, and earth, and seas,
   Conspire to lift Thy glories high,
   And speak Thine endless praise.
   ISAAC WATTS.

TWINE THE GARLAND.

Arranged.

ALFRED G. MORTIMER, B.D.

1. Twine the Easter gar - land, Deck the grave with flow'rs, Je-sus Christ hath
2. Like a might-y vic - tor Rose the Lord that morn, Brighter light and
3. Faith, a ray of glo - ry, Shows the emp-ty tomb, And the man - y

con - quered Death's enthrall-ing pow'rs; Sa-tan, sin, and sor - row,
pur - er On this earth was born: Rays of hope and mer - cy,
man - sions Of the Saviour's home, Where the saints were resting,

Lie beneath His feet; Christians, raise your voices, Sing His tri-umph sweet.
Round His form were shed, Scattered doubt and show-ered Glo-ry on the dead.
Aft-er death and grave :— Christians, we can conquer, Sing His pow'r to save.

CHORUS.

Twine the Eas - ter gar - land, Deck the grave with flow'rs,

Je - sus Christ hath con - quered Death's enthrall-ing powers

BLESSED SAVIOUR.

Tune: Twine the Garland.

1. Saviour, blessed Saviour,
   Listen whilst we sing,
   Hearts and voices raising
   Praises to our King.
   All we have we offer,
   All we hope to be,
   Body, soul, and spirit,
   All we yield to Thee.

2. Nearer, ever nearer,
   Christ, we draw to Thee,
   Deep in adoration
   Bending low the knee:
   Thou for our redemption
   Cam'st on earth to die;
   Thou, that we might follow,
   Hast gone up on high.

3. Great and ever greater
   Are Thy mercies here,
   True and everlasting
   Are the glories there,
   Where no pain, or sorrow,
   Toil, or care, is known,
   Where the angel-legions
   Circle round Thy throne.

GODFREY THRING.

EVER ONWARD.

Tune: Twine the Garland.

1. Brighter still and brighter
   Glows the western sun,
   Shedding all its gladness
   O'er our work that's done.
   Time will soon be over,
   Toil and sorrow past,
   May we, blessed Saviour,
   Find a rest at last.

2. Onward, ever onward,
   Journeying o'er the road
   Worn by saints before us,
   Journeying on to God;
   Leaving all behind us,
   May we hasten on,
   Backward never looking
   Till the prize is won.

3. Higher then and higher
   Bear the ransomed soul,
   Earthly toils forgotten,
   Saviour, to its goal;
   Where in joys unthought of
   Saints with angels sing,
   Never weary raising
   Praises to their King.

THRING.

CHRISTIAN SOLDIERS.

Tune: Twine the Garland.

1. Onward Christian soldiers,
   Marching as to war,
   With the cross of Jesus
   Going on before.
   Christ, the royal Master,
   Leads against the foe;
   Forward into battle,
   See His banners go.

2. Like a mighty army,
   Moves the church of God;
   Brothers, we are treading
   Where the saints have trod.
   We are not divided,
   All one body we,
   One in hope and doctrine,
   One in charity.

3. Crowns and thrones may perish,
   Kingdoms rise and wane,
   But the church of Jesus
   Constant will remain.
   Gates of Hell can never
   'Gainst that church prevail;
   We have Christ's own promise,
   And that cannot fail.

4. Onward then, ye faithful,
   Join our happy throng,
   Blend with ours your voices,
   In the triumph-song:
   Glory, laud, and honor,
   Unto Christ the King;
   This, thro' countless ages,
   Men and angels sing.

S. BARING-GOULD.

SWEET HOME.

Tune; Song of the Angels.

1. Oh, my sweet home, Jerusalem!
    Thy joys when shall I see?
The King that sitteth on thy throne
    In his felicity?
Thy gardens and thy goodly walks
    Continually are green,
Where grow such sweet and pleasant
    flowers,
    As nowhere else are seen.

CHORUS.

O mother dear, Jerusalem!
    When shall I come to thee?
When shall my sorrows have an end?
    Thy joys when shall I see?

2. Right through thy streets with pleasing
    sound,
    The flood of life doth flow;
And on the banks, on either side,
    The trees of life do grow.
Those trees each month yield ripened
    fruit;
    For evermore they spring,
And all the nations of the earth,
    To thee their honors bring.

QUARLES.

HEAVENWARD.

Tune: Song of the Angels.

1. Give me the wings of faith to rise
    Within the veil, and see
The saints above, how great their joys,
    How bright their glories be,
Once they were mourning here below,
    And wet their couch with tears;
They wrestled hard, as we do now,
    With sin and doubt and fears.

CHORUS.

Our glorious Leader claims our praise
    For His own pattern given,
While the long cloud of witnesses
    Show the same path to heaven.

2. I asked them whence their vict'ry came
    They, with united breath,
Ascribe their conquest to the Lamb,
    Their triumph to His death.
They marked the footsteps that He tro
    His zeal inspired their breast,
And following their incarnate God,
    Possessed their promised rest.

ISAAC WATTS.

SONG OF THE ANGELS.

E. H. SEARS.　　　　　　　　FRANK M. DAVIS.

Moderato.

1. Calm on   the list'ning   ear of night, Come heaven's melodious strains,
2. The answer-ing hills of   Pal-es-tine, Send back the glad re-ply;

SONG OF THE ANGELS. Concluded.

Where wild Ju - de - a stretch - es far Her sil - ver mantled plains.
And greet, from all their ho - ly heights The day-spring from on high.

Ce - les - tial choirs, from courts a-bove, Shed sa - cred glo - ries there,
O'er the blue depths of Gal - i - lee There comes a ho - lier calm,

And an - gels with their sparkling lyres, Wake music on the air.
And Shar - on waves in sol - emn praise, Her silent groves of Palm.

CHORUS. *Animated.*

ff "Glo - ry to God," the sounding skies Loud with their anthems ring,

Peace to the earth, good will to men, From heaven's eter - nal King!

SONG OF VICTORY.

J. DAMASCENE.

BERTHOLD TOURS.

1. The Day of Res - ur - rec - tion! Earth, tell it out a - broad;
2. Our hearts be free from e - vil, That we may see a - right
3. Now let the heav'ns be joy - ful! Let earth her song be - gin!

The Pass - o - ver of glad - ness, The Pass - o - ver of God.
The Lord in rays e - ter - nal Of res - ur - rec - tion light;
Let the round world keep tri - umph, And all that is there - in!

From death to life e - ter - nal, From this world to the sky,
And, list - 'ning to His ac - cents, May hear so calm and plain
In - vis - i - ble and vis - i - ble Their notes let all things blend,

Our Christ has bro't us o - ver With hymns of vic - to - ry.
His own "All hail!" and hear - ing May raise the vic - tor strain.
For Christ the Lord hath ris - en, Our joy that hath no end. A-MEN.

* Tune Aurelia may be used to this hymn if preferable.

DAY OF REST.

Tune: Song of Victory.

1. O day of rest and gladness,
    O day of joy and light,
O balm of care and sadness,
    Most beautiful, most bright!
On thee the high and lowly
    Before the eternal throne,
Sing, Holy, Holy, Holy,
    To God the three in one.

2. On thee at the creation,
    The light first had its birth;
On thee for our salvation
    Christ rose from depths of earth;
On thee our Lord victorious
    The Spirit sent from heaven;
And thus on thee most glorious
    A triple light was given.

3. Thou art a cooling fountain
    In life's dry, weary sand;
From thee, like Pisgah's mountain,
    We view the promised land:
A day of sweet refection,
    A day of holy love,
A day of resurrection
    From earth to things above.

4. To-day on weary nations
    The heavenly manna falls;
To holy convocations
    The silver trumpet calls;
Where gospel light is glowing
    With pure and radiant beams,
And living waters flowing
    With soul-refreshing streams.

5. New graces ever gaining
    From this our day of rest,
We reach the rest remaining
    To spirits of the blest;
To Holy Ghost be praises,
    To Father and to Son;
The church her voice upraises
    To Thee, blest three in one.

C. WORDSWORTH.

HEAVENLY LOVE.

Tune: Song of Victory.

1. In heavenly love abiding,
    No change my heart shall fear,
And safe is such confiding,
    For nothing changes here:
The storm may roar without me,
    My heart may low be laid,
But God is round about me,
    And can I be dismayed?

2. Wherever He may guide me,
    No want shall turn me back;
My Shepherd is beside me,
    And nothing can I lack;
His wisdom ever waketh,
    His sight is never dim;
He knows the way He taketh,
    And I will walk with Him.

3. Green pastures are before me
    Which yet I have not seen;
Bright skies will soon be o'er me
    Where darkest clouds have been;
My hope I cannot measure,
    My path in life is free:
My Saviour has my treasure,
    And He will walk with me.

A. L. WARING.

THE WATCHERS.

Tune: Song of Victory.

1. The watchers on the mountain
    Proclaim the Bridegroom near;
Go meet Him as He cometh
    With hallelujahs clear;
The marriage feast is waiting,
    The gates wide open stand;
Up! up! ye heirs of glory,
    The Bridegroom is at hand.

2. Our Hope and Expectation,
    O Jesus! now appear;
Arise, thou Sun so longed for!
    O'er this benighted sphere;
With hearts and hands uplifted,
    We plead, O Lord! to see
The day of earth's redemption,
    That brings us unto Thee.

L. LAURENTE.

ONWARD WE COME.

Geo. C. Hugg.
CORNET.

Ciro Pinsuti.

On-ward we come, Sing-ing with glee;

Christ hath a-ris - en, from death's bondage free, Where grave, oh where

Thy vic - to - ry; Je - sus my Sav-iour liv - eth for me.

NOTE. The words to this beautiful processional should be committed to memory, and sung until school is seated.

HE IS RISEN.

Spirited.
GIRLS.

ALL.

Geo. C. Hugg.

Christ, the Lord, is risen to-day! He is risen in - deed!

GIRLS. ALL.

Christ, the Lord, is risen to - day, He is risen in - deed.

SEMI CHORUS.

"He cap-tive led cap-tiv - i- ty, He robbed the grave of vic - to-ry," He
Let ev -'ry liv-ing soul rejoice, And sing with one u - nit - ed voice, The
The great and glorious work is done, Free grace to all through Christ, the Son; Ho-

broke the bars of death, He broke the bars of death.
Sav - iour rose to - day, The Sav-iour rose to - day.
san - na to His name, Ho - san - na to His name.

FULL CHORUS.

Halle - lu- jah, hal-le - lu -jah, Halle - lu-jah, hal-le - lu-jah, Halle-

lu - jah, hal - le - lu - jah, The Lord is risen in - deed!

EASTERTIDE.

H. B. McKeever.   Jno. R. Sweney.

DUET.

1. Now the burst-ing spring a-wakes, Now the flow-ers bloom,
2. Now the birds are fly-ing home, Sing-ing as they come;
3. Man-y lov'd-ones sweet-ly sleep In their lone-ly tombs,

Now the sleep-ing in-sects creep From their low-ly tomb.
Now the world is full of joy, Eas-ter-tide has come.
Where the an-gels keep their watch Till the Sav-iour comes.

CHORUS.

Ring the chimes! ring the chimes! On this hap-py Easter day.
Ring them merri-ly! ring them merri-ly!

Ring the chimes! ring the chimes! On this hap-py day.
Ring them merri-ly! ring them merri-ly!

RING GLAD BELLS.

A. S. DOUGHTY.
CIRO PINSUTI.

Joyously.

1. O ring the glad bells, The joy telling bells, In praise of our Lord in Bethlehem born,
2. O ring the glad bells, The life cheering bells, In chorus of praise to Emmanuel ring;
3. Ring, ring the glad bells, Their music dispels The shadows of gloom that darken [the way,

Where manger and stall Held Monarch of all, In poverty's garments for-lorn.
Whom prophets foretold, And patriarchs old Revealed as the Heaven-born King.
Ring out and proclaim The wonderful name, Make joyful this bright natal day.

CHORUS.

Then ring the glad bells, Keep ringing the bells, While myriad voices the glad chorus [swells

With glo-ry to God, good-will unto men, For Jesus the Saviour is born.

PEACE ON EARTH.

Geo. C. Hugg.   Rob't. Finch.

Con allegrezza.

1. A song of joy pervades the air, Break forth ye bells in ring - ing;
2. Come bow be - fore the King of kings, In Man - ger cra-dle ly - ing;

Sweet hal - le - lu - jahs ev' - ry where, And ho - ly angels sing - ing,
Un - to the world great joy he brings, And saves us all from dy - ing.

Chorus. *ff*

Glo - ry, glo - ry in the highest ! Glo - ry, glo - ry in the high - est.

Solo or Semi-Chorus.
dolce.

Peace on earth .... good-will to men, ... Christ is

born .... in Beth-le - hem, ... Peace on earth .... good-will to

PEACE ON EARTH. Concluded.

marcato.

men, ... Christ is born .... in Beth-le-hem.

Glo-ry, glo-ry in the high-est! Glo-ry, glo-ry in the high-est!

rallentando. *ff*

Glo-ry, glo-ry in the high-est, Re-peat the song a-gain.

WONDROUS GRACE.

Tune: Dennis.

1. Behold what wondrous grace
   The Father hath bestowed
   On sinners of a mortal race,
   To call them sons of God !

2. 'Tis no surprising thing
   That we should be unknown,
   The Jewish world knew not their King,
   God's everlasting Son.

3. Nor doth it yet appear
   How great we must be made;
   But when we see our Saviour here,
   We shall be like our Head.

4. A hope so much divine
   May trials well endure,
   May purge our souls from sense and sin,
   As Christ, the Lord, is pure.

5. If in my Father's love
   I share a filial part,
   Send down Thy Spirit like a dove
   To rest upon my heart.

6. We would no longer lie
   Like slaves beneath the throne;
   Our faith shall "Abba, Father!" cry,
   And Thou the kindred own.

ON JESUS.

Tune: Jerusalem, the Golden.

1. I lay my sins on Jesus,
   The spotless Lamb of God;
   He bears them all and frees us
   From the accursed load ;
   I bring my guilt to Jesus,
   To wash my crimson stains
   White in His blood most precious
   Till not a spot remains.

2. I lay my wants on Jesus;
   All fullness dwells in Him;
   He heals all my diseases,
   He doth my soul redeem ;
   I lay my griefs on Jesus,
   My burdens and my cares;
   He from them all releases,
   He all my sorrows shares.

3. I long to be like Jesus,
   Meek, loving, lowly, mild;
   I long to be like Jesus,
   The Father's holy child ;
   I long to be with Jesus,
   Amid the heavenly throng,
   To sing with saints His praises,
   To learn the angels' song.

REJOICE!

GEO. C. HUGG.

GEO. C. HUGG.

Sing and re-joice all ye peo-ple, Christ is ris - en!

Christ is ris - en! Sing and re-joice all ye peo - ple!

1 For death is vanquished now; **2** death is vanquished now.

SEMI—CHORUS.
Male voices, 1st time loud, Female voices, 2d time soft.

He has ris'n......... triumphant o'er His foes! Hal-le lu - jah!

Christ the Lord to life a-rose; He has ris'n......... tri-umph-ant

REJOICE. Concluded.

o'er His foes; Yea He rose, our dear Sav - iour, a - rose, rose.

FULL CHORUS.

Sing and rejoice all ye peo - ple! Sing and rejoice all ye peo - ple!

Sing and rejoice all ye peo - ple! For death is vanquished now;

Sing and rejoice all ye peo - ple! Christ is ris - en! Christ is ris - en!

Sing and rejoice all ye peo - ple! To Christ the Vic - tor bow.

CAROL, SWEETLY CAROL.

Arr. by G. C. H.   Rev. H. G. Batterson, D. D.

1. Car - ol, sweet-ly car - ol, The Sav-iour rose to - day:
2. Car - ol, sweet-ly car - ol, The tomb is emp - ty now,
3. Car - ol, sweet-ly car - ol, This hap - py East - er time;

Bear the joy - ful tid - ings, Oh, bear them far a - way.
Je - sus Christ hath ris - en, Each knee to Him shall bow.
Hark! the bells are peal - ing Their res - ur - rec - tion chime;

Car - ol, sweet-ly car - ol, Till earth's re - mot - est bound
Car - ol, sweet-ly car - ol, Your joy and love pro - claim,
Car - ol, sweet-ly car - ol, Ye shin - ing ones a - bove,

Shall hear the might-y cho - rus And ech - o back the sound.
Death's ter-rors all are vanquished, The Sav-iour lives a - gain.
And sing in loud-est num - bers, Oh, sing re-deem-ing Love.

CAROL, SWEETLY CAROL.—Concluded.

CHORUS.

Car - ol, sweet-ly car - ol, Car - ol sweet-ly to - day.
Car - - ol, car - ol,

Car - ol, car - ol, car - ol sweet-ly to - day.

Bear the joy - ful tid - ings, Oh, bear them far a - way.

ALMIGHTY KING.

Tune: Italian Hymn.

1. Come, Thou Almighty King!
   Help us Thy name to sing,
   Help us to praise;
   Father! all-glorious,
   O'er all victorious,
   Come and reign over us,
   Ancient of Days!

2. Come, holy Comforter!
   Thy sacred witness bear
   In this glad hour;
   Thou who almighty art!
   Now rule in every heart,
   And ne'er from us depart,
   Spirit of power!

3. To the great one in three
   The highest praises be,
   Hence evermore;
   His sovereign majesty
   May we in glory see,
   And to eternity
   Love and adore.

NATIVE LAND.

Tune: America.

1. God bless our native land!
   Firm may she ever stand
   Through storm and night;
   When the wild tempests rave,
   Ruler of winds and wave!
   Do thou our country save
   By Thy great might.

2. For her our prayer shall rise
   To God above the skies,
   On Him we wait;
   Thou who art ever nigh,
   Guardian with watchful eye!
   To Thee alone we cry,
   God save the State.

3. Our fathers' God! to Thee,
   Author of liberty,
   To Thee we sing;
   Long may our land be bright
   With freedom's holy light;
   Protect us by Thy might,
   Great God, our King!

ON THEE.

HORATIUS BONAR.   GEO. C. HUGG.
Slowly.

1. On Thee, O Je - sus, strongly lean-ing, I calm - ly on - ward go;
2. True Light of light, for-ev - er shin-ing, I hail Thy hap-py ray;
3. In Thee my soul is sweet - ly rest-ing, My hand takes hold of Thine,
4. My hope, my joy, my peace, my glo-ry, My first, my last, my all;

No cloud, no cold - ness in - ter-ven-ing, To damp love's blessed glow,
Bright Sun of suns, still un - de-clin-ing, 'Tis Thou who mak'st my day!
My hope is ev - er upward hast-ing, And Thou, and Thou, art mine!
Great theme of the un-end - ing sto-ry In yon ce - les - tial hall.

In Thee for-ev - er, Lord, a - bid-ing, I feel that all is well;
Without Thee life and time are sadness; No fragrance breathes a-round;
My ref' - uge from each storm that ra-ges, From wind, and wave, and war,
Great theme a-bove of song and wonder In a - ges yet to come,

With-in Thy love for-ev - er hiding, Who can my gladness tell?
But with Thee e - ven grief is gladness, My heart its home hath found.
My home throughout e - ter - nal a - ges, A-bove yon sparkling star!
True theme be - low while here we wander, A - las, how cold and dumb!

WE'LL NEVER SAY GOOD-BYE.

Geo. C. Hugg.   Geo. C. Hugg.

1. In the morn of morns when we all meet there, In the home far above the sky;
2. Never sadness there, neither grief, nor tear, In that fair shining home on high!
3. With our kindred dear, in that love-light clear, While the long rolling ages fly,

We'll rehearse the scenes we have left behind, But we never will say "good-bye."
But they swell the song, happy ransomed throng; And they never will say "good-bye."
We will meet, and greet, at the Saviour's feet, But we never will say "good-bye."

CHORUS.

In the dawn - ing of the morn - ing, In that home far a-bove the sky;
In the dawning clear of the morning fair,

Hap-py meet - ing, hap-py greet - ing, When we never say "good-bye."
Happy meeting there, hap-py greeting there,

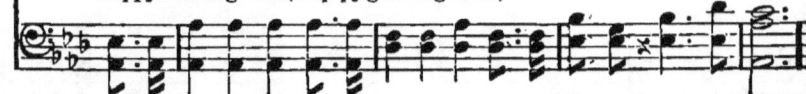

GEO. C. HUGG.

GEO. C. HUGG.

1. There's a great hap - py throng by the bright Jas - per sea! And there's
2. In that land, neith - er glow of the can - dle, or sun, Lights the
3. Nev - er fear, breth-ren dear, if the Lord should ap-pear, Say - ing,

more ev - en now, crossing o - ver! And their theme is the love of the
way of the host crossing o - ver! Ho - ly rays from the face of our
haste, join your friends crossing o - ver! 'Twill be sweet, there to greet, at the

Lamb that was slain, And a greet - ing to those cross - ing o - ver!
God, and the Lamb, Guide the feet of our friends cross - ing o - ver!
dear Saviour's feet All our friends that are done cross - ing o - ver!

CHORUS.

Hal - le - lu - jah! Hal - le - lu - jah! hear the sweet flow - ing song

Of the great ransomed throng, In their lays they are prais - ing the

Lamb that was slain, And are greet-ing their friends crossing o - ver.

LIGHT OF DAY.

GEO. W. DOANE.
p Slow.

JOSEPH BARNBY.

1. Soft - ly now the light of day Fades up - on my sight a - way;
2. Thou, whose all - per - vad - ing eye Naught es-capes, with-out, within,
3. Soon for me the light of day Shall for - ev - er pass a-way;

cres.   *dim.*   *rit.*

Free from care, from la - bor free, Lord, I would com-mune with Thee.
Par - don each in - firm - i - ty, O - pen fault and se - cret sin.
Then, from sin and sor-row free, Take me, Lord, to dwell with Thee.

FOR ME!

J. B. ATCHINSON.

GEO. C. HUGG.

1. Oh what a sin-ner I have been, Yet Je-sus died for me!
2. How oft have I provoked the Lord, Yet Je-sus died for me!
3. And can it be, what I have heard, The Sa-viour died for me?

My sin-ful life the Lord hath seen, Yet Je-sus died for me!
Ig-nored the teachings of His word, Yet Je-sus died for me!
For me, who hath His wrath incurred, The Sa-viour died for me!

I shun'd His grace, His mercy spurned, His love refused and from Him turned,
Un-heed-ed oft the still small voice, Sweeter than bird of Par-a-dise,
Ah, yes, the lost to seek and save, His pre-cious life He freely gave;

Yet o'er my soul He long hath yearned, For Je-sus died for me!
And still my heart cannot re-joice, Tho' Je-sus died for me!
"And cries to ev-'ry sin-bound slave," I died, I died for thee!

HORATIUS BONAR.

GEO. C. HUGG.

1. Hark! 'tis the watch-man's cry, "Wake, breth - ren, wake!"
2. Call to each wake-ing band, "Watch, breth - ren, watch!"
3. Heed we the stew - ard's call, "Work, breth - ren, work!"
4. Sound now the fin - al chord! "Praise, breth - ren, praise!"

Je - sus him-self is nigh, "Wake, breth - ren, wake!"
Clear is our Lord's com - mand, "Watch, breth - ren, watch!"
There's room e - nough for all, "Work, breth - ren, work!"
Thrice ho - ly is the Lord; "Praise, breth - ren, praise!"

Sleep is for sons of night; Ye are the chil - dren of
Be ye as men that wait, Al - ways at their Mas - ter's
This vine-yard of the Lord, Con - stant la - bor will af -
What more be - fits the tongues, Soon to lead the an - gel's

light; Yours is the glo - ry bright; "Wake, brethren, wake!"
gate, E'en tho' He tar - ry late; "Watch, brethren, watch!"
ford; He will your work re - ward; "Work, brethren, work!"
songs, While heav'n the note pro - longs? "Praise, brethren, praise!"

ON JESUS.

HORATIUS BONAR.   JOSEPH BARNBY.

Slow, smooth, and tenderly.

1. I lay my sins on Je - sus, The spot - less Lamb of God;
2. I lay my wants on Je - sus, All full - ness dwells in Him;
3. I rest my soul on Je - sus, This wea - ry soul of mine:
4. I long to be like Je - sus, Meek, lov - ing, low - ly, mild;

He bears them all, and frees us From the ac - curs - ed load:
He heals all my dis - eas - es, He doth my soul re - deem;
His right hand me em - brac - es, I on His breast re - cline:
I long to be like Je - sus, The Fath-er's ho - ly Child!

I bring my guilt . to Je - sus, To wash my crim - son stains
I lay my griefs on Je - sus, My bur - dens and my cares:
I love the name of Je - sus, Im - man - uel, Christ, and Lord;
I long to be like Je - sus, A - mid the heav - 'nly throng,

White in   His blood most pre - cious, Till not a   spot re - mains.
He from them all re - leas - es, He all my sor - rows shares.
Like fra-grance on the breez - es, His Name a - broad is poured.
To sing with saints His prais - es, To learn the au - gel's song.

E. R. LATTA.   CHAS. K. LANGLEY.

1. I will go to Je-sus now, (just now,) For He calls and bids me
2. I will go to Je-sus now, (just now,) While He speaks in voice so
3. I will go to Je-sus now, (just now,) And no long-er wait-ing

come; (bids me come;) I will seek His smil-ing face, (His face,)
kind; (so kind;) In my child-hood I will go, (will go,)
stand; (waiting stand;) He'll ac-cept of me, I know, (I know,)

REFRAIN.

And from Him would nev-er roam; (never roam;) } I will go to
"They who ear-ly seek, shall find;" (shall find;) } Je-sus,
And will hold me by the hand. (the hand.) } I will

Je-sus now, To Je-sus now, To
go to Je-sus now, go to Je-sus now,
go to Je-sus now, To Je-sus now, To

Je-sus now;
Go to Je-sus now; I will go to Je-sus now.
Je-sus now;

By permission.

72

SUNSHINE OF HIS LOVE.

LAURA E. NEWELL.   CHAS. K. LANGLEY.

Joyously.

1. In the sun-shine of His love, let us live, let us live, Let us
2. In the sun-shine of His love, we may roam, we may roam, And the
3. In the sun-shine of His love, we'll a - bide, we'll a - bide, Tho' the

la - bor in the light of His cross, of His cross; We may
days will bring us com - fort and peace, and peace, Till He
time on earth be brief, or be long, or be long, Till He

run life's race with joy all the way, all the way, If we
call us to His dear, bliss - ful home, bliss-ful home,Where the
bears us to the land o'er the tide, o'er the tide,Where we'd

count the joy of earth on-ly dross. In the sun-shine of His love we'll a -
wea-ry from their toils have release. We may feel His ten-der love in our
praise Him with the glad ransomed throng. In the sun-shine of His love let us

bide, we'll a-bide, Till the vic-to-ries of life all are won, all are won,
hearts, in our hearts,He will lead us all the way by the hand, by the hand,
die, let us die, May the ev - er-last-ing arms then en-fold, then en-fold,

By permission.

With His bless-ed word to coun - sel and guide, and guide, We'll not
For He loves with com-pas - sion di - vine, di - vine, And will
May He bear us to His king-dom on high, on high, To His

REFRAIN.

wea-ry till the con - flict is done. ⎫ In the sunshine of His love, we may
guide us to the bright, better land. ⎬
pal-ace in the cit - y of gold. ⎭ In the sunshine of His

stay, we may stay, And His words shall be a lamp un - to our
love, we may stay, And His word shall be a

feet, un - to our feet, And will guide us un - to heav'n's per-fect
lamp,

day, per-fect day, When the work we have to do is com-plete, is complete.

SATISFIED.

HORATIUS BONAR.   GEO. C. HUGG.

1. When I awake in the sweet morn of morns, After whose dawning night ne'er returns:
2. When I shall meet with the ones I have lov'd, Clasp in my arms the long, long remov'd,
3. When I shall gaze on the dear face of Him, Who died for me, with eye no more dim,

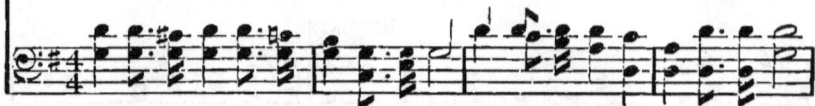

And with whose glory the day ev - er burns, I shall be sat - is - fied.
And find how faithful the Lord then has proved, I shall be sat - is - fied.
And praise Him ever with heaven's swelling hymn, I shall be sat - is - fied.

CHORUS.

I shall be sat - is - fied; I shall be sat - is - fied;
I shall be satisfied, I shall be satisfied,

When in the like-ness of God I'm ar-rayed, I shall be sat - is - fied.

GEO. C. HUGG.

GEO. C. HUGG.

1. When this poor heart is burdened with grief, No-bod-y knows like Je-sus!
2. When on the mount of joy and de-light, No-bod-y knows like Je-sus!
3. All that I am, or ev-er shall be, No-bod-y knows like Je-sus!

When at the Cross I cry for re-lief, No-bod-y knows like Je-sus!
When faith up-lifts to mansions so bright, No-bod-y knows like Je-sus!
All there remains in glo-ry for me, No-bod-y knows like Je-sus!

CHORUS.

No-bod-y knows like Je-sus! No-bod-y knows like Je-sus!

Precious Re-deem-er, Brother and Friend, No-bod-y knows like Je-sus!

SEND ME LIGHT.

Horatius Bonar.

Geo. C. Hugg.

1. Lord, give me light to do Thy work, For on - ly, Lord, from Thee
2. The way is nar - row, of - ten dark, With lights and shadows strewn:
3. Oh, send me light to do Thy work! More light, more wis-dom give;
4. The work is Thine, not mine, O Lord; It is Thy race we run;

Can come the light, by which these eyes The way of life can see.
I wan - der oft, and think it Thine, When walking in my own.
Then shall I work Thy work in - deed, While on Thine earth I live.
Give light! and then shall all I do, Be well and tru - ly done.

CHORUS.

Send me light! send me light! Light a-long the toilsome way!
Send me light, send me light,

Send me light, dear Lord, that I may labor on, Till I rest in e - ter-nal day.

F. R. HAVERGAL.

GEO. C. HUGG.

1. Thro' the yes - ter-day of a - ges, Je - sus, Thou hast been the same;
2. Joy-ful-ly we stand and wit-ness, Thou art still to - day the same;
3. Gaz - ing down the great for-ev - er, Bright-er glows the one sweet Name,

Thro' our own life's chequered pa - ges, Still the one dear changeless name,
In Thy per - fect, glo - rious fit-ness, Meet-ing ev' - ry need and claim,
Stead-fast ra-diance, pal - ing nev - er, Je - sus, Je - sus! still the same,

Well may we in Thee con - fide, Faith-ful Sav - iour, proved and tried.
Chief - est of ten thous-and, Thou ! Sav - iour, O, most pre - cious now !
Ev - er-more Thou shalt en - dure, Our own Sav - iour, strong and sure.

CHORUS.

Just the same Je - sus! The ver - y same Je - sus!

Thro' the cease-less, roll - ing a - ges, Je - sus, Thou art still the same.

NO CANDLE, NOR SUN.

GEO. C. HUGG. GEO. C. HUGG.

1. I have read of a won-der-ful cit-y, Whose in-
2. There's a throne in the midst of that cit-y, From which
3. By the banks of that life-giv-ing Riv-er, Stands the
4. In that far-a-way home, up in glo-ry, Which the

hab-i-tants nev-er grow old; And whose walls gleam with bright shining
flow-eth a pure crys-tal stream; They that drink of its life-giv-ing
Tree, that in E-den did bloom; And its leaves are for heal-ing of
Sav-iour has gone to pre-pare; We'll re-peat, o'er and o'er, the Old

jew-els, While its streets glow with bur-nished gold.
wa-ter, Clothe their souls in e-ter-nal gleam.
na-tions, While its fruit, cur-eth mor-tal gloom.
Sto-ry, And will share all the beau-ties there.

CHORUS.

"And they need no can-dle, neith-er light of the sun, And they need no can-dle, neither light of the sun; And they need no

can-dle, neither light of the sun; For the Lamb is the light there-of."

SUN OF MY SOUL.

J. KEBLE.   W. H. MONK.

1. Sun of my soul, thou Sav-iour dear! It is not night if Thou be near;
2. When soft the dews of kind-ly sleep My wearied eye-lids gent-ly steep,
3. A-bide with me from morn till eve, For without Thee I can-not live;
4. Come near to bless us when we wake, Ere through the world our way we take,

Oh may no earth-born cloud a-rise To hide Thee from Thy servant's eyes.
Be my last thought, how sweet to rest For ev-er on my Saviour's breast!
A-bide with me when night is nigh, For without Thee I dare not die.
Till in the o-cean of Thy love We lose our-selves in heav'n a-bove.

RESTING.

F. R. HAVERGAL.   GEO. C. HUGG.

1. Rest-ing on the faithful-ness of Christ our Lord;   Rest-ing on   the
2. Rest-ing 'neath His guiding hand for un-seen days;   Rest-ing 'neath His
3. Rest-ing in the for-tress while the foe is nigh;   Rest-ing in   the
4. Rest-ing in the pastures, and be-neath the Rock;   Rest-ing by   the

full-ness of His own sure word;   Rest-ing on His pow-er, on His
shad-ow from the noon-tide rays;   Rest-ing at the e - ven - tide be-
life-boat while the waves roll high;   Rest-ing in His Char-iot for the
wa - ters where He leads His flock;   Rest-ing, while we lis-ten, at His

love un - told;   Rest-ing on His cov - e - nant se - cured of old.
neath His wing,   In the fair pa - vil - ion of our Sa - viour King.
swift glad race;   Rest-ing, al - ways rest-ing in His bound-less grace.
glo - rious feet;   Rest-ing in His ver - y arms! O rest com - plete!

CHORUS.

Rest-ing and be-liev-ing, let us on - ward press, Rest-ing on Him-self the Lord our Righteousness; Rest - ing and re - joic - ing, let His

saved ones sing, Glo - ry, glo - ry, glo - ry be to Christ our King.

MY SHEPHERD.

HORATIUS BONAR. HANDEL.

1. Je - ho - vah He my shepherd is, I shall have neither want nor ill;
2. This soul of mine He lift-eth up, And me He lead-eth gent-ly on,
3. Yea, and when walking in the vale Of death's dark shade, I fear no ill;
4. A ta - ble Thou hast rich-ly spread, For me mine en - e - mies be-fore;
5. Good-ness and mer-cy all the days Of my life here shall fol-low me,

In pas - tures green He lays me down, And leads me by the wa-ters still.
A - long the paths of righteousness; And all for His name's sake a - lone.
For Thou art ev - er with me Lord; Thy rod and staff they com-fort still.
With oil Thou dost a-noint my head, My cup with blessings runneth o'er.
And then for length of end - less days, My home Je-ho-vah's house shall be.

UNDER HIS SHADOW.

F. R. HAVERGAL.

GEO. C. HUGG.

SOLO.

With feeling.

1. Sit down be-neath the shad - ow, And rest with great de - light;
2. Bring ev - 'ry wea - ry bur - den, Thy sin, thy fear, thy grief;
3. A lit - tle while, tho' part - ed, Re-mem-ber, wait, and love,

DUET.

The faith that now be-holds Him, Is pledge of fu - ture sight,
He calls the heav-y la - den, And gives them kind re - lief.
Un - til He comes in glo - ry, Un - til we meet a - bove;

CHORUS.

Our Mas-ter's love re - mem - ber, Ex-ceed-ing great and free;
His right-eous-ness all glo - rious, Thy fes-tal robe shall be;
Till in the Fa-ther's king - dom, The heav'n-ly feast is spread,

Lift up your heart in glad - ness, For He re-mem-bers thee.
And love that pass-eth knowl-edge, His ban-ner o - ver thee.
And we be-hold His beau - ty, Whose blood for us was shed.

F. R. HAVERGAL.   GEO. C. HUGG.

1. No-bod-y knows but Je-sus!   Is   it not bet-ter   so,
2. No-bod-y knows but Je-sus!   My Lord, I bless Thee now,
3. No-bod-y knows but Je-sus!   How great my tri-als be,
4. No-bod-y knows but Je-sus!   'Tis mu-sic for to - day,

That no one else but Je-sus,   My own dear Lord, should know?
I feel Thee draw-ing near-er,   As 'neath the cross I   bow.
And noth-ing else can help me,   Like His sweet sym-pa - thy.
And thro' e - ter-nal a - ges,   'Twill chime a - long the way.

CHORUS.

No-bod-y knows but Je-sus!   Low at His feet I   bow,

And there I tell my grief and joy, That no one knows but Thou.

SONG OF LOVE.

Arr. by Geo. C. Hugg.

A. H. Brown.

Moderato.

f

Solo.

p

1. I will love Thee, O, my treas-ure; I will love Thee, O, my strength;
2. I will praise Thee, Sun of Glo - ry, For Thy beams have gladness brought;
3. Be my heart more warm-ly glow-ing, Sweet and pure the songs I raise;

I will love Thee, with - out meas- ure, And will love Thee right at length;
I will praise Thee, will a - dore Thee, For the light I vain - ly sought;
And in love, and ar - dor grow-ing, Let me sing a - new Thy praise:

cres.

I will love Thee, Light di - vine, Till I die and find Thee mine.
Praise Thee, that Thy words so blest, Speak my troub-led soul to rest.
Near to Thee, and near - er still, Draw this heart, this mind, this will.

CHORUS.

I will love in joy or sor-row, I will love Thee

long and well, I will love to-day, to-mor-row,

While I in this bod-y dwell, I will love Thee,

Light di-vine! Till I die and find Thee mine.

LIGHT DIVINE.

Geo. C. Hugg.   Geo. C. Hugg.

Joyously.

1. There is sun-light in my soul, bless-ed sun-light! Cheering up life's darksome
2. There is sun-light in my soul, bless-ed sun-light! Love and praise beyond con-
3. There is sun-light in my soul, bless-ed sun-light! Sure 'twill guide me safely

way;   Oh the bless-ed Lord of life, is that sun - light, Bless-ed
trol,   Oh the bless-ed Lord of life, is that sun - light, Bless-ed
home, Oh the bless-ed Lord of life, is that sun - light, Bless-ed

Chorus.

sun-light, of the soul.   I am walk-ing in the light, bless-ed
sun-light, of the soul.
sun-light, of the soul.

sun - light! Where the clouds of love divine o'er me roll;   Oh, the

Blessed sun-light!   o'er me roll;

sun - light, bless-ed sun - light, Glorious sunlight of the soul.

Oh, the sun-light,   Blessed sun-light,

BEYOND.

HORATIUS BONAR. GEO. C. HUGG.

1. Be-yond the smil-ing and the weeping, I shall be soon;
2. Be-yond the blooming and the fad-ing, I shall be soon;
3. Be-yond the part-ing and the meeting, I shall be soon;
4. Be-yond the frost-chain and the fev-er, I shall be soon;

Be-yond the wak-ing and the sleeping, Be-yond the sow-ing
Be-yond the shin-ing and the shading, Be-yond the hop-ing
Be-yond the fare-well and the greeting, Be-yond the pul-se's
Be-yond the rock-waste and the riv-er, Be-yond the ev-er

and the reaping, I shall be soon.
and the dreading, I shall be soon.
fev-er beat-ing, I shall be soon.
and the nev-er, I shall be soon.

Love, rest, and home!

Home, sweet, sweet Home! Lord tar-ry not, but come!

* This composition may be sung as Chorus throughout.

COME TO ME.

HORATIUS BONAR.

GEO. C. HUGG.

1. I heard the voice of Je-sus say, "Come un-to Me and rest! Lay
2. I heard the voice of Je-sus say, "Be-hold, I free-ly give The
3. I heard the voice of Je-sus say, "I am this dark world's Light; Look

down, thou weary one, lay down Thy head up-on My breast!" I came to
liv-ing wa-ter, thirst-y one! Stoop down, and drink and live;" I came to
un-to Me; thy morn shall rise, And all thy day be bright;" I looked to

Je-sus as I was; Wear-y and worn, and sad; I found in Him a
Je-sus, and I drank Of that life-giv ing stream; My thirst was quench'd, my
Je-sus, and I found In Him, my Star, my Sun; And in that light of

rest-ing place, And He has made me glad: And He has made me glad.
soul re-vived, And now I live in Him; And now I live in Him.
life I'll walk, Till trav'ling days are done; Till trav-'ling days are done.

THINE.

F. R. HAVERGAL.

GEO. C. HUGG.

1. Take my life and let it be, Con - se - cra - ted, Lord, to Thee;
2. Take my feet and let them be, Swift and beau - ti - ful for Thee;
3. Take my lips and let them be, Filled with mes - sa - ges for Thee;
4. Take my mo- ments and my days, Let them flow in end-less praise;
5. Take my will and make it Thine; It shall be no long-er mine;
6. Take my love, my Lord, I pour At Thy feet its treas-ure store!

Take my hands and let them move, At the im - pulse of Thy love.
Take my voice and let me sing, Al - ways, on - ly for my King.
Take my sil - ver and my gold,—Not a mite would I with-hold.
Take my in - te - lect, and use Ev -'ry pow'r as Thou shalt choose.
Take my heart it is Thine own,—It shall be Thy roy - al Throne.
Take my - self, and I will be, Ev - er, on - ly, all for Thee.

CHORUS.

All I am, or hope to be; Con - se - crate me Lord to Thee:

Seal me with Thy blood di - vine, Make me ev - er, on - ly Thine.

FRESH SPRINGS.

F. R. HAVERGAL.

GEO. C. HUGG.

1. Springs of life in des-ert pla-ces, Shall thy God un-seal for thee;
2. Springs of sweet re-fresh-ment flowing, When thy work is hard or long;
3. Springs of peace, when conflict heightens, Thine up-lift-ed eye shall see;
4. Springs of com-fort, strangely springing, Thro' the bit-ter wells of woe;

Quick'ning and re-viv-ing gra-ces, Dew like, heal-ing, sweet and free.
Cour-age, hope, and pow'r be-stow-ing, Lightening la-bor with a song.
Peace that strengthens, calms and brightens, Peace it-self a vic-to-ry.
Founts of hid-den gladness bringing, Joy that earth can ne'er be-stow.

CHORUS.

Hear thy Fa-ther's bless-ed prom-ise! List-en, thirst-y, wea-ry
Hear thy Father's blessed promise! List-en, thirsty, wea-ry

one! "I will pour my Ho-ly Spir-it, On thy cho-sen seed, O Son."

Helen Marion Burnside.　　　　　　　　　Geo. C. Hugg.

1. Call-est Thou thus, oh Mas - ter? Call-est Thou thus to me?
2. Com-est Thou thus, oh Mas - ter? Com-est Thou thus to me?
3. "Child," said the gracious Mas - ter, With voice di - vine - ly sweet,

Wea-ry and heav - y la - den, Long-ing to come to Thee,
Un-trimm'd, my lamp, and dy - ing, And house not meet for Thee,
I on - ly ask a wel - come; Rest, for my wea - ry feet!

Out in the lone - ly dark - ness Thy dear voice sounds so sweet,
Thou art so great and ho - ly, I am by sin un - done,
Come o'er my low - ly thresh-old, Dark, and de - filed by sin,

ritard.

I am not wor - thy Master, oh no, Not wor-thy to kiss Thy feet.
I am not wor - thy Master, oh no, Not worthy that Thou should'st come.
Tho' all unwor - thy Master, oh come, I pray Thee, come, en - ter in.

SINGING FOR JESUS.

F. R. HAVERGAL.

GEO. C. HUGG..

1. Singing for Je - sus, our Saviour and King, Sing-ing for Je - sus, the
2. Singing for Je - sus, and trying to win Ma-ny to love Him, and
3. Singing for Je - sus, our Life and our Light; Sing-ing for Him as we
4. Singing for Je - sus, our Shepherd and Guide, Singing for glad - ness of

Lord whom we love; All ad - o - ra - tion we joy-ons-ly bring,
join in the song; Call-ing the wrong and the wan-der-ing in,
press to the mark; Singing for Him when the morning is bright,
heart that He gives; Singing for won - der and praise that He died,

CHORUS.

Longing to Praise as we'll praise Him a - bove.
Rolling the cho-rus of glad-ness a - long.
Singing, still singing for Him in the dark.
Singing for blessing and joy that He lives.

Sing-ing for Je - sus,

Sing - ing for Je - sus, Sing - ing, Sing - ing, all day long;

Singing for Je-sus, Singing for Je-sus, Singing, singing, E - den songs.

F. R. HAVERGAL.
Expressione.

GEO. C. HUGG.

1. Leave be-hind earth's empty pleas-ure, Fleet-ing hope and changeful love;
2. Leave be-hind thy faithless sor - row, And thy ev - ery an - xious care

Leave its soon cor - ro - ding treas-ure, There are bet - ter things a-bove.
He who on - ly knows the mor-row, Can for thee its bur-dens bear.

Leave, Oh, leave thy fond as - pir - ings, Bid thy rest - less heart be still,
Leave the dark-ness gath'ring o'er thee, Leave the sha - dow-land be- hind;

Cease, Oh, cease thy vain de - sir - ings, On - ly seek thy Fa-ther's will.
Realms of glo - ry lie be-fore thee; En - ter in, and wel-come find.

WALK IN THE LIGHT.

BERNARD BARTON.   GEO. C. HUGG.

1. Walk in the light! so shalt thou know That fel-low-ship of love, His
2. Walk in the light! and thou shalt find Thy heart made tru-ly His, Who
3. Walk in the light! and e'en the tomb No fear-ful shade shall wear; Glo-
4. Walk in the light! thy path shall be Peace-ful, se-rene, and bright; For

spir-it on-ly can be-stow,   Who reigns in light a-bove.
dwells in cloud-less light en-shrined,   In whom no dark-ness is.
ry shall chase a-way its gloom,   For Christ has con-quered there.
God by grace, shall dwell in thee,   And God him-self is light.

CHORUS.

Walk.......... in the light!.............. Walk........... in the
Walk in the light, in the beautiful light of God! Walk in the light, in the

light!......................   Walk...................... in the
beau-ti-ful light of God!   Walk in .the light in the

light!...................   Walk in the beau-ti-ful light of God.
beau-ti-ful light of God!

F. R. HAVERGAL.   GEO. C. HUGG.

1. I am trust-ing Thee, Lord Je - sus, Trust-ing on - ly Thee.
2. I am trust-ing Thee for cleans-ing, In the crim-son flood.
3. I am trust-ing Thee for pow - er; Thine can nev - er fail!

Trust-ing Thee for full sal - va - tion Great and free.
Trust-ing Thee to make me ho - ly By Thy blood.
Words which Thou Thy-self shalt give me, Must pre - vail.

I am trusting Thee for par - don! At Thy feet I bow,
I am trusting Thee to guide me, Thou a - lone shalt lead!
I am trusting Thee Lord Je - sus; Nev - er let me fall!

For thy grace and ten - der mer - cy, Trust - ing now.
Ev' - ry day and hour sup - ply - ing All my need.
I am trust - ing Thee for ev - er, And for all.

THIS SAME JESUS.

F. R. HAVERGAL.
Earnestly.

GEO. C. HUGG.

1. This same Je-sus! Oh! how sweetly   Fall those words up-on the ear,
2. He who wand'red, poor and homeless,   By the stor-my Gal-i-lee;
3. He who gent-ly call'd the wea-ry,   'Come and I will give you rest!'
4. This same Je-sus! when the vis-ion   Of that last and aw-ful day,

Like a swell of far off mu-sic   In a night-watch still and drear!
He who on the night-robed mountain Bent in prayer the wea-ried knee;
He who loved the lit-tle chil-dren, Took them in His arms and blest;
Bursts up-on the prostrate spir-it,   Like a mid-night light-ning ray;

He who healed the hopeless lep-er,   He who dried the wid-ows' tear;
He who spake as none had spoken,   An-gel-wis-dom from a-bove,
He, the lone-ly Man of sor-rows, 'Neath our sin-curse bend-ing low;
Then, we lift our hearts a-dor-ing This same Je-sus! loved and known,

He who changed to life and gladness   Help-less suff'-ring, trem-bling fear.
All-for-giv-ing, ne'er up-braiding,   Full of ten-der-ness and love.
By His faithless friends forsak-en   In the dark-est hours of woe.
Him, our own most gracious Saviour,   Seat-ed on the great white Throne.

CHORUS.

This same Je-sus! this same Je-sus! Bless - ed be His ho - ly name;

Yes - ter-day, to-day, for - ev - er ; Je - sus Christ is still the Same.

BONAR.

HORATIUS BONAR,   GEO. C. HUGG.

1. Je - ho - vah is   my light and hope,Whom there-fore fear shall I?
2. Let hosts a - gainst me pitch their camp, My heart no fear shall feel,
3. One thing I   of   Je - ho - vah sought,For this still do   I   pray;
4. My help in days past Thou hast been; Do not for -sake me now;
5. Oh wait up - on Je - ho - vah, wait, Be firm and strong, he will

Je - ho - vah is   my strength and life Who shall me ter - ri - fy?
Let war   a - gainst me rise, in   this My trust a - bid - eth still.
That in   Je - ho - vah's house a - bide For - ev - er - more I may.
Nor leave me, O   my God, the God' Of   my sal - va - tion Thou.
Strength-en the faint - ness of thy heart,Wait on Je - ho - vah still.

ONLY REMEMBERED.

HORATIUS BONAR.　　　　　　　　　　　　　　　　GEO. C. HUGG.

1. Up and a-way, like the dew of the morning, Soaring from earth to its
2. Shall I be missed if an - oth - er succeed me, Reaping the fields I in
3. On - ly the truth that in life I have spok-en, On - ly the seed that on
4. Oh! when the Saviour shall make up His jewels, When the bright crowns of re-

home in the sun; Thus would I pass from the earth and its toil-ing,
spring-time have sown? No, for the sow - er may pass from his la - bors,
earth I have sown, These shall pass onward when I am for-got - ten,
joic - ing are won, Then will His faithful and wea - ry dis - ci - ples

CHORUS.

On - ly remember'd by what I have done.
On - ly remember'd by what he has done.　} On - ly remembered, Yes
Fruits of the harvest, and what I have done.
All be remember'd by what they have done.

on - ly remembered; On - ly remembered by what I have done:

Only remembered, Yes, only remembered, Only remembered, By what I have done.

CHRIST BE PRAISED.

E. CASWELL.   J. BARNBY.

1. When morning gilds the skies, My heart a - wak - ing cries,
2. Does sad - ness fill my mind? A sol - ace here I find,
3. The night be - comes as day, When from the heart we say,
4. In heaven's e - ter - nal bliss The love - liest strain is this,

May Je - sus Christ be praised! A - like at work and prayer,
May Je - sus Christ be praised! Or fades my earth - ly bliss?
May Je - sus Christ be praised! The pow'rs of dark - ness fear,
Let Je - sus Christ be praised! Let earth and sea, and sky,

To Je - sus I re - pair; May Je - sus Christ be praised!
My com - fort still is this, May Je - sus Christ be praised!
When this sweet chant they hear, May Je - sus Christ be praised!
From depth to heigth re - ply, May Je - sus Christ be praised!

THE WORKER'S PRAYER.

F. R. HAVERGAL.

GEO. C. HUGG.

1. Lord, speak to me, that I may speak In liv-ing ech-oes of Thy tone;
2. O lead me, Lord, that I may lead The wand'ring and the wav'ring feet;
3. O teach me, Lord, that I may teach The precious things Thou dost impart;
4. O fill me with Thy fullness, Lord, Un-til my ver-y heart o'er flow

As Thou hast sought, so let me seek Thy err-ing chil-dren, lost and lone.
O feed me, Lord, that I may feed Thy hung'ring ones with manna sweet.
And wing my words, that they may reach The hidden depths of many a heart.
In kindling thought and glowing word, Thy love to tell, Thy praise to show.

CHORUS.

O use me, Lord, use e-ven me, Just as Thou wilt, and when, and where,

Un-til Thy bless-ed face I see, Thy rest, Thy joy, Thy glo-ry share.

LOOKING UNTO JESUS.

F. R. HAVERGAL. ROBT. FINCH.

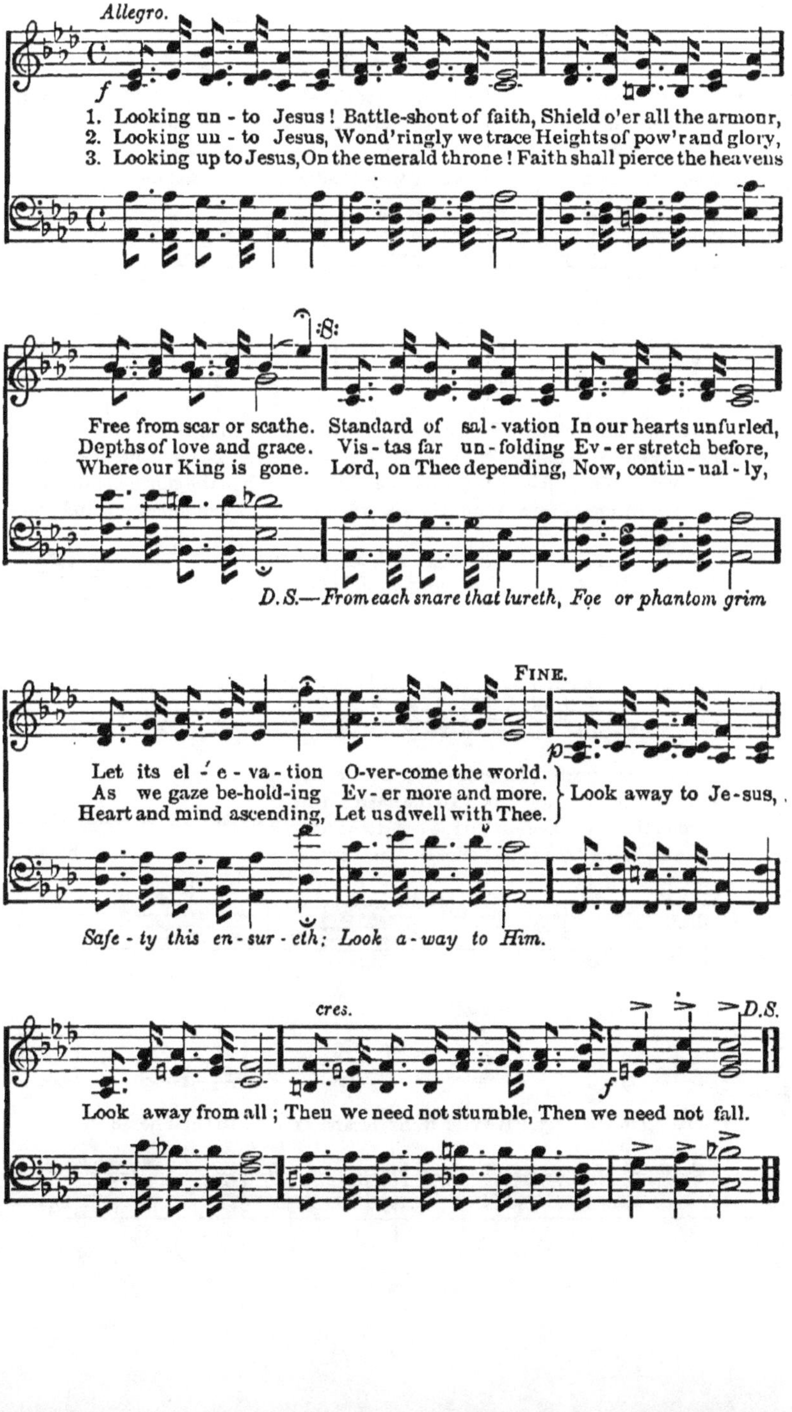

T. J. POTTER.

JOHNSON BARKER.

1. Brightly gleams our banner, Pointing to the sky, Waving wand'rers onward
2. Je-sus, Lord, and Master, At thy sa-cred feet, Here with hearts rejoicing,
3. All our days di-rect us, In the way we go, Lead us on vic-to-rious
4. Then with Saints and Angels May we join above, Offering end-less prais-es

To their home on high; Journeying o'er the desert, Glad-ly thus we pray,
See thy children meet; Oft-en have we left Thee, Oft-en gone a-stray,
O-ver ev-ery foe; Bid thine angel shield us, When the storm-clouds lower,
At thy throne of love; When the toil is o-ver, Then comes rest and peace,

CHORUS.

And with hearts united, Take our heav'nward way.
Keep us, mighty Sav-iour, In the narrow way.
Pardon thou and save us In the last dread hour.
Je-sus, in his beauty;—Songs that never cease.

Brightly gleams our banner,

Point-ing to the sky, Waving wand'rers on-ward To their home on high.

HOSANNA IN THE HIGHEST.

GEO. C. HUGG.

ROB'T. FINCH.

Marcato vivace.

Ho - san - na in the highest! Ho - san - na in the highest! A

King has come to reign! All glorious is His fame! The news abroad proclaim! Im-

man-uel is His name, He comes on earth, in peace, and love, to reign!

Re - joice, re - joice, the might - y King has come! He
Re - joice, re - joice, the might - y King has come! "The

* This Chorus for each verse.

HOSANNA IN THE HIGHEST. Continued.

left His glad a - bode, A - midst the heav'n-ly throng; Re -
i - ron fet - ters yield, The gates of brass un - fold! Re -

joice, re - joice, Sal - va - tion now ap-pears, Re -
joice, re - joice, The pris - 'ner now is free, And

(GIRLS.) ad lib.

joice and praise His name.............. in song!
nam,e His Holy name,
sin-ful bonds no long - - er hold!
long-er hold, no long -

p

Ped.

We come, we come, we come with glad acclaim! The
We come, we come, we come with glad acclaim! The

Saviour promised long, Has come on earth to reign, We come, we come, re-
song of praise and love, Breaks forth from ev'ry tongue, We come, we come, re-

Finale.

joic-ing in His name! Hosanna in the highest sing. Hosanna to Jesus' name.
joic-ing in His name! Hosanna in the highest sing. Hosanna to Jesus' name

* Play 8 last bars as interlude.

THE MASTER IS COME.

HORATIUS BONAR.   GEO. C. HUGG

Slowly.

1. The Mas-ter is come, and call-eth ! He speaketh in grace to Thee ;
2. He comes for the great re-ward-ing, Of la - bor here for Him done ;
3. The Bridegroom is come, and calleth ! He comes, He can wait no more ;
4. The Judge is now come, and calleth ! Be - fore Him the sons of men ;

O dost thou not hear Him call-ing, A - rise ye and fol - low me.
He crowneth His faith-ful ser-vants With His ev - er-last - ing crown.
He comes for the marriage sup-per, The mar - ri - age joy in store.
Long, long has His voice been sounding, It sounds for the lost a - gain.

CHORUS.

A - rise, and fol - low me quickly, Thus He giv-eth the loud command ;

A - rise, and as-cend in brightness In - to that glo - rious land.

HORATIUS BONAR. GEO. C. HUGG.

1. Life is com-ing, death is go-ing, E - ven so, A - men!
2. Love is com-ing, hate is go-ing, E - ven so, A - men!
3. Cells are burst-ing, chains are break-ing, E - ven so, A - men!
4. Graves are open-ing, dead are meet-ing, E - ven so, A - men!

Quick-ly past us time is flow-ing, E - ven so, A - men!
Seeds of u - ni - ty are sow-ing, E - ven so, A - men!
Wea - ry spir - its cease their ach-ing, E - ven so, A - men!
Heaven and earth each oth - er greet-ing, E - ven so, A - men!

Day is dawn-ing, night is fly-ing, E - ven so, A - men!
Fear is pass-ing, hope is bright'ning, E - ven so, A - men!
Tears are dry-ing, songs are break-ing, E - ven so, A - men!
Hill and vale put on their glad-ness, E - ven so, A - men!

Soon shall end this grief and sigh-ing, E - ven so, A - men!
Burdened brows and hearts are light'-ning, E - ven so, A - men!
Earth's glad ech-oes are a - wak-ing, E - ven so, A - men!
Not a trace re - mains of sad-ness, E - ven so, A - men!

HAVE YOU NOT A WORD.

F. R. HAVERGAL.   GEO. C. HUGG.

Joyously.

1. Have you not a word for Je - sus?   Not a word to say for Him?
2. He has spoken words of bless - ing,   Pardon, peace, and love to you,
3. Have you not a word for Je - sus?   Will the world His praise proclaim?
4. Have you not a word for Je - sus?   Some, perchance while ye are dumb,

He is listening thro' the cho - rus   Of the burning Ser - a - phim!
Glorious hope and gracious com - fort,   Strong and tender, sweet and true;
Who will speak if ye are si - lent?   Ye who know and love His name.
Wait and weary for your mes - sage,   Hop-ing you will bid them come,

He is listening; does He hear you   Speak-ing of the things of earth,
Does He hear you telling oth - ers   Something of His love un - told,
You, whom He hath called and chosen   His own wit - nesses to be,
Nev - er telling hidden sor - rows,   Lingering just outside the door,

On - ly of its passing pleas - ure,   Self - ish sorrow, empty mirth?
O - ver-flowings of thanksgiv - ing   For His mercies man - i - fold?
Will you tell your gracious Mas - ter,   Lord we cannot speak for Thee.
Longing for your hand to lead them   In - to rest for ev - er-more.

F. R. HAVERGAL.

GEO. C. HUGG.

1. Yes, we have a word for Je - sus! Liv - ing echoes we will be,
2. Ma - ny ef - forts it may cost , us, Ma - ny heart-beats, many a fear,
3. Yes, we have a word for Je - sus! We will bravely speak for Thee,
4. Help us lov-ing-ly to la - bor, Look - ing for Thy present smile,

Of Thine own sweet words of blessing, Of Thy gracious come to me,
But Thou knowest, and will strengthen, And Thy help is always near ;
And Thy bold and faithful sol - dier, Saviour, we would henceforth be :
Look-ing for Thy promised blessing, Thro' the bright'ning, little while ;

Je - sus, Master! Yes, we love Thee, And to prove our love would lay,
Give us grace to fol-low ful - ly, Vanquish-ing our faithless shame,
In Thy name set up our ban - ners, While Thine own shall wave above,
Words for Thee in weakness spoken, Thou wilt here ac-cept and own,

Fruit of lips which Thou wilt o - pen, At Thy blessed feet to - day.
Fee - bly it may be, but tru - ly Wit-ness-ing for Thy dear name.
With Thy crimson name of mer-cy, And Thy golden name of love.
And confess them in Thy glo - ry, When we see Thee on Thy throne.

RICH IN BLESSING.

JAS. ALLEN.

GEO. C. HUGG.

Fervently.

1. Sweet the moments, rich in blessing, Which be-fore the cross I spend;
2. Tru-ly bless-ed is this sta-tion, Low be-fore His cross to lie,
3. Here it is I find my heaven, While up-on the Lamb I gaze;
4. Love and grief my heart di-vid-ing, With my tears His feet I bathe;

Life and health, and peace possesing, From the sin-ner's dy-ing Friend.
While I see di-vine compassion, Beam-ing from His lov-ing eye.
Love I much, I've much forgiven; I'm a mir-a-cle of grace.
Con-stant still in faith a-bid-ing, Life de-riv-ing from His death.

CHORUS.

Rich in blessing! rich in blessing! Moments at the cross I spend;

Tru-ly bless-ed is this sta-tion, Low be-fore the cross to bend.

F. R. HAVERGAL.
Slowly.

GEO. C. HUGG.

1. Is it for me, dear Sav-iour, Thy glo-ry and Thy rest?
2. Is it for me to list-en To Thy be-lov-ed voice,
3. O Sav-iour, pre-cious Sav-iour, My heart is at Thy feet;

For me, so weak and sin-ful, Oh shall I thus be blessed?
And hear its sweet-est mu-sic Bid e-ven me re-joice?
I bless Thee, and I love Thee, And Thee I long to meet.

Is it for me to see Thee In all Thy glo-rious grace?
Is it for me, Thy wel-come, Thy gra-cious en-ter in?
A thrill of sol-emn glad-ness Has hushed my ver-y heart,

And gaze in end-less rapt - ure, On Thy be-lov-ed face.
For me, Thy "Come, ye bless - ed!" For me, so full of sin?
To think that I shall real - ly Be-hold Thee as Thou art.

THE LORD IS KING.

J. CONDER.   GEO. C. HUGG.

1. The Lord is King!............   lift up thy voice,............
2. The Lord is King!............   who then shall dare...........
3. The Lord is King!............   Child of the dust,............
4. He reigns! ye Saints............   ex - alt your strains;........

The Lord is King!   lift up thy voice,
The Lord is King!   who then shall dare
The Lord is King!   child of the dust,
He reigns! ye Saints   exalt your strains;

O earth, and all ye heav'ns re-joice! From world to world the joy shall ring,
Re - sist His will, dis-trust His care, Or mur-mur at His wise de - crees,
The Judge of all the earth is just: Ho - ly and true are all His ways;
Your God is King, your Father reigus; And He is at the Fath-er's side,

CHORUS.

The Lord Om-nip - o - tent is King. The Lord is King,............
Or doubt His roy - al prom-i - ses?
Let ev-'ry creature speak His praise.
The Man of Love, the cru- ci - fied.

The Lord is King,

The Lord is King,............   Re- joice! re-joice the Lord is King,

The Lord is King,

Arr. by GEO. C. HUGG.

GEO. C. HUGG.

Spirited.

1. O my sweet home, Je - ru - sa - lem! Thy joys when shall I see?
2. Thy gar - dens and thy good - ly walks, Con - tin - ual - ly are green,
3. Right thro' thy streets with pleasing sound, The flood of life doth flow;
4. O Moth - er dear, Je - ru - sa - lem! When shall I come to thee?

The King that sit - teth on thy throne, In His fe - lic - i - ty?
Where grow such sweet and pleasant flowers, As no-where else are seen.
And on the banks, on eith - er side, The trees of life do grow.
When shall my sor - rows have an end? Thy joys when shall I see.

CHORUS.

Way o - ver Jor - dan! Way o - ver Jor - dan! O

land of rest, and bliss un - told, My own e - ter - nal home.

GALILEE.

Robert Morris, LL. D.

Geo. C. Hugg.

Slow and feelingly.

1. Each coo-ing dove............ and sigh-ing bough,............
2. Each flowr'-y glen............ and mos-sy dell,............
3. And when I read............ the thrill-ing love,............

Each coo-ing dove
Each flowr'y glen
And when I read

and sigh-ing bough,
and mos-sy dell,
the thrill-ing love,

That makes the eve............ so blest to me,............
Where hap-py birds............ in song a-gree,............
Of Him who walked............ up-on the sea,............

That makes the eve
Where hap-py birds
Of Him who walked

so blest to me,
in song a-gree,
up-on the sea,

Has some-thing far............ di - vin-er now,............
Thro' sun-ny morn............ the prais-es tell,............
I long, O, how............ I long once more,............

Has something far
Thro' sun-ny morn
I long, O, how

di - vin-er now,
the prais-es tell,
I long once more,

It bears me back............ to Gal - i - lee,............
Of sights, and sounds............ in Gal - i - lee,............
To fol-low Him............ in Gal - i - lee,............

It bears me back
Of sights, and sounds
To fol-low Him

to Gal - i - lee,
in Gal - i - lee,
in Gal - i - lee,

REFRAIN.

O Gal - i - lee,.................... sweet Gal - i - lee,....................
O Gal - i - lee, sweet Gal - i - lee,

Where Je - sus loved.................. so much to be,....................
Where Je - sus loved so much to be,

O Gal - i - lee,.................... sweet Gal - i - lee,....................
O Gal - i - lee, sweet Gal - i - lee,

Come sing thy song.................... a - gain to me....................
Come sing thy song a - gain to me.

FORWARD!

Arr. by GEO. C. HUGG.

ROBERT FINCH.

1. Forward go!—and let the strain Tell of tri-umph yet a-gain;
2. Forward go, de-spond no more! Je-sus calls, and goes. be-fore!
3. Forward go!—the saints a-bove; Still pro-long the strain of love,

For the Lord, who reigns on high, Leads His own to vic-to-ry:
He will guard His cho-sen bride, He will nev-er leave her side:
Soon may we, with-in the gate, See with them our King in state:

Thro' the world's op-pos-ing might, Thro' the gath'ring gloom of night;
King-doms flour-ish, and de-cay, Heav'n and earth will pass a-way;
There will He His choir u-nite, All ar-rayed in robes of white;

Strong in faith let ho-ly song, Cheer us as we march a-long.
Ev-er-more our voic-es raise, Songs of triumph, joy and praise.
There will songs of pur-est joy, All their bliss-ful life em-ploy.

GEO. C. HUGG.

Fervently.

GEO. C. HUGG.

1. Hark! I hear my Sav-iour say, Wea-ry child, lean on Me;
2. In thy weak-ness heed the call, Wea-ry child, lean on Me;
3. O - ver Jor - dan's chilling stream, Wea-ry child, lean on Me;

Smooth will be thy on - ward way, Lean, my child, on Me.
Sim - ply trust - ing, that is all, Lean, my child, on Me.
See, be-yond, the home-land gleam, Lean, my child, on Me.

I will strengthen, love and cheer, In the night or day-light clear;
Like a lone and wea · ry dove, Thee I'll shel - ter from a - bove;
Friends and loved-ones shall u - nite In that realm of glo - ry bright,

Still - ing doubts, or gloom-y fear, Lean, my child, on Me.
"God is wis - dom, God is love," Lean, my child, on Me.
In that E - den land of light, Lean, my child, on Me.

OUR REFUGE.

M. E. SERVOSS.

GEO. C. HUGG.

1. Our God is our ref - uge and strength, What then have His children to fear?
2. Our God is our ref - uge and strength, From trouble on sea and on land ;
3. Our God is our ref - uge and strength, Our en - e - mies He will o'er throw,
4. Ex - alt Him ! ye children of light, While o'er you His banners shall wave ;

Though mountains be cast in the sea, Yet we know that the Father is near.
He will never forsake those who trust The om - nip - o - tent power of His hand.
He is with us in mercy and pow'r, In His strength we can conquer each foe.
Sing His prais-es a - bove all His works, Lord Jehovah, al-might-y to save.

CHORUS.

Our God is our ref-uge and strength, Oh ! trust Him, what ever be - fall ;

He'll shield us from all that can harm, And deliv-er when-ev-er we call.

F. R. HAVERGAL. GEO. C. HUGG.

Joyously.

1. Like a riv-er glo-rious, Is God's perfect peace, O - ver all vic - to - rious,
2. Hidden in the hol - low, Of His blessed hand, Nev - er foe can fol - low,
3. Ev-'ry joy or tri - al, Fall-eth from above, Traced upon our di - al,

In its bright increase; Per - fect yet it flow-eth Full-er ev-'ry day;
Nev - er trai-tor stand, Not a surge of wor - ry, Not a shade of care,
By the sun of love, We may trust Him solely, All for us to do;

Perfect yet it groweth Deeper all the way.
Not a blast of hur-ry, Touch the spirit there. } Stay'd upon Je - ho - vah,
They who trust Him wholly, Find Him wholly true.

CHORUS.

cres.

Hearts are ful-ly blest, Finding as He promised perfect peace and rest.

PRECIOUS SAVIOUR.

F. R. HAVERGAL.

DR. ARTHUR S. HOLLOWAY.

1. O Sa - viour, precious Sa - viour, Whom yet un - seen we love;
2. O bring - er of sal - va - tion, Who won-drous-ly hast wrought,
3. In Thee all ful - ness dwell - eth, All grace and pow'r di - vine;
4. O grant the con - sum - a - tion, Of this our song a - bove,

O name of might and fa - vor, All oth - er names a - bove!
Thy - self the rev - e - la - tion Of love be - yond our thought!
The glo - ry that ex - cell - eth, O Son of God, is Thine:
In end - less ad - o - ra - tion, And ev - er - last - ing love:

mp

We wor - ship Thee, we bless Thee, To Thee a - lone we sing;
We wor - ship Thee, we bless Thee, To Thee a - lone we sing;
We wor - ship Thee, we bless Thee, To Thee a - lone we sing;
Then shall we praise and bless Thee, Whose perfect prais - es ring;

cres.

We praise Thee, and con - fess Thee Our Ho - ly Lord and King.
We praise Thee, and con - fess Thee Our gracious Lord and King.
We praise Thee, and con - fess Thee Our glo - rious Lord and King.
And ev - er - more con - fess Thee Our Saviour and our King.

CHORUS.

O Sa - viour, pre - cious Sa - viour, Whom yet un - seen we love,

O name of might and fa - vor, All oth - er names a - bove.

IT IS NOT DYING.

C. MALAN.   M. MOSES.

1. No, no, it is not dy-ing To go un-to our God ; This gloomy earth for-
2. No, no, it is not dy-ing Heav'n's citizen to be ; A crown immortal
3. No, no, it is not dy-ing To hear this gracious word, Receive a Father's
4. No, no, it is not dy-ing The shepherd's voice to know, His sheep He ever
5. No, no, it is not dy-ing To wear a lordly crown ; Among God's people
6. Oh, no, it is not dying, Thou Saviour of mankind : There streams of love are

sak - ing, Our jour-ney homeward taking A - long the star-ry road.
wearing, And rest un-bro-ken shar-ing, From care and conflict free.
blessing, For ev - er-more pos-ses-sing The fa - vor of the Lord.
lead-eth, His peace-ful flock He feed-eth, Where liv-ing pastures grow.
dwelling, The glo - rious triumph swelling Of Him whose sway we own.
flow-ing, No hindrance ev - er knowing ; Here drops a-lone we find.

WHO IS ON THE LORD'S SIDE?

HAVERGAL, (Arranged.)   · GEO. C. HUGG.

With spirit.

1. Who is on the Lord's side, Who will serve the King?
2. Not for weight of glo - ry, Not for crown of palm,
3. Je - sus, Thou hast bought us, Not with gold or gem,
4. Fierce may be the con - flict, Strong may be the foe,

Who will join His ar - my, Oth - er lives to bring? Who will leave the
En - ter we this ser-vice, And for con-flict arm ; But for love that
But with Thine own life-blood, For Thy di - a - dem ; Arm-ing with Thy
But the King's own army, None can o - ver-throw ; Round His standard

world's side? Who will face the foe? Who is on the Lord's side
claim - eth Lives for whom He died, He whom Je - sus nam - eth
Spir - it, All who come to Thee, They are thus made will - ing,
press - ing, Vic - t'ry is se - cure, For His truth, un - chang-ing,

CHORUS.

Who for Him will go?
Must be on His side.
They are thus made free.
Makes the triumph sure.
} Who is on the Lord's side, Who will serve the King?

Who will be His help-ers, Other lives to bring? By Thy love and mercy

By Thy grace divine, We are on the Lord's side ; Saviour, we are Thine.

MERCY.

STOCKER. GOTTSCHALK.

1. Gra - cious Spir-it ! Love di-vine ! Let Thy light with - in me shine ;
2. Speak Thy pard'ning grace to me, Set the burdened sin - ner free ;
3. Life and peace to me im-part, Seal sal - va - tion on my heart,
4. Let me nev - er from Thee stray, Keep me in the nar - row way ;

All my guilt-y fears re - move, Fill me with Thy heav'nly love.
Lead me to the Lamb of God, Wash me in His pre - cious blood.
Breathe Thyself in - to my breast, Earn-est of im-mor-tal rest.
Fill my soul with joy di - vine, Keep me, Lord ! for ev - er Thine.

COMING OF THE HEALER.

F. R. Havergal.   Geo. C. Hugg.

1. When light di-vine had touched the hills by slumb'ring Gal-i - lee,
2. And then they brought the suffering ones, the lone-ly, or the dear,
3. He heard the prayer, and gave the will and strength to touch the hem,
4. O ten - der One, O might-y One, who nev - er sent a - way,

The gold-en wave must roll a - far to -wards the west-ern sea;
And laid them at the Heal - er's feet, from far a - way, or near;
And gave the faith, and vir - tue flow - ed from Him, and healed them;
The sin - ner or the suf - fer-er, Thou art the same to - day!

And when the men had knowledge of the Ho - ly One of God,
Then bent be - fore the Wondrous One, and earn - est-ly be - sought,
For ev - 'ry one whose fee-blest touch thus met the Sa - viour's pow'r,
The same in love, the same in pow'r, and Thou art wait - ing still,

Then they went forth thro' all the land, and spread His fame a - broad.
That they might on - ly touch the hem a - round His garment wrought.
Rose up in per - fect health and strength in that ac-cept-ed hour.
To heal the mul - ti - tude that come, yea, who-so-ev - er will.

CHORUS.

O sing of the Lov-ing One! O sing of the Heal-ing One!

O sing of the Might-y One! Re-deem-er, Sav-iour, King.

SEYMOUR.

HAMMOND.　　　　　　　　　　　　　VON WEBER.

1. Lord! we come be - fore Thee now, At Thy feet we humbly bow;
2. Lord, on Thee our souls de-pend, In com-pas-sion, now de-scend;
3. In Thine own ap - point - ed way, Now we seek Thee, here we stay;
4. Send some mes-sage from Thy word, That may joy and peace af - ford;

Oh! do not our suit dis-dain! Shall we seek Thee, Lord! in vain?
Fill our hearts with Thy rich grace, Tune our lips to sing Thy praise.
Lord! we know not how to go, Till a bless - ing Thou be-stow.
Let Thy Spir-it now im - part Full sal - va - tion to each heart.

FORTH TO THE FIELD.

J. E. HALL.   J. E. HALL.

1. The har-vest-field is now a-wait-ing, All whit-ened
2. The lab'-rers are so few in num-ber, The field so
3. The har-vest-time will soon be o-ver, Then for-ward

for the sic-kle keen, Go forth then, lab'-rers, to the
large and ver-y white; I fear some grain will go un-
to the field to-day, And toil with earn-est, strong en-

reap-ing, And gath-er quick the rip-ened grain.
gar-nered, Then let us work with all our might.
deav-or To gar-ner grain while now we may.

CHORUS.

Forth! to the field! Forth! to the field, And garner grain while time shall last; Forth!

to   the field, Forth!to   the field, Be - fore the harvest days are past.

ABIDE WITH ME.

H. F. LYTE.   W. H. MONK.

1. A - bide with me; fast falls the e - ven - tide; The   dark-ness
2. Not a brief glance I beg, a   pass - ing word, But   as Thou
3. I   need Thy pres - ence ev' - ry pass - ing hour; What but Thy
4. Hold Thou Thy Cross be - fore my clos - ing eyes, Shine through the

deep - ens: Lord, with me a - bide! When oth - er   help - ers
dwell'st with Thy dis - ci - ples, Lord, Fa - mil - iar, con - de -
grace can foil the temp-ter's pow'r? Who like Thy - self my
gloom, and point me to the skies: Heav'n's morning breaks, and

fail, and comforts flee, Help of the helpless, oh, a - bide with   me.
scending, pa-tient, free, Come, not to sojourn, but a - bide with   me.
guide and stay can be? Thro' cloud and sunshine, oh, a - bide with   me.
earth's vain shadow's flee; In   life, in death; O Lord, a - bide with   me.

TO THE RESCUE!

F. A. B.

F. A. BLACKMER.

1. See! a sail a-mid the fear-ful breakers Yon-der, waving sig-nals
2. High-er, fierc-er yet the tem-pest ra-ges, Can the life-boat live in
3. See the forms un-to the old wreck clinging, Now they beckon to the
4. Sin is rampant and its bil-lows rag-ing, And these human wrecks are
5. Go and tell them Christ has died to win them, Bid them cast on Him their

of dis-tress; Haste! make read-y at the sav-ing sta-tion
such a sea? Yes, for God who rules the storm shall guide it,
shore for aid; Now their cry for help your ears if greet-ing!
ev-'ry-where; Broth-er, do not lose a sin-gle mo-ment
load of care; Bid them hope, tho' 'neath the wave now sink-ing

CHORUS.

Man the life-boat, praying God to bless!
Till imperilled souls in safe-ty be.
Sure-ly you would not the call e-vade.
Heaven's message to them quickly bear.
Tell them Christ can save e-ven there.

To the res-cue, to the res-cue!

Brother, seize the oar! Launch the life-boat, launch the life-boat! Pull away from shore! Speed the life-boat, speed the life-boat! Brave the wind and wave!

To the res-cue, to the res-cue! Pre-cious souls to save.

SABBATH EVE.

ELLERTON.   LOCKHART.

1. The day of praise is done; The eve-ning shad-ows fall;
2. Around Thy throne on high, Where night can nev-er be,
3. Too faint our an-thems here; Too soon of praise we tire;
4. Shine Thou with-in us, then, A day that knows no end,

Yet pass not from us with the sun, True Light that light'nest all!
The white-robed harpers of the sky, Bring cease-less hymns to thee.
But oh, the strains how full and clear Of that e-ter-nal choir!
Till songs of an-gels and of men In per-fect praise shall blend.

HE HATH DONE IT.

F. R. HAVERGAL.

GEO. C. HUGG.

Fervently.

1. Sing, O heav'ns! the Lord hath done it! Sound it forth o'er land and sea!
2. Lis - ten now! the Lord hath done it! For He loved us un - to death;
3. O be - lieve the Lord hath done it! Wherefore lin-ger? wherefore doubt?

Je - sus says I have re - deemed thee, Now re-turn, re-turn to me;
It is fin-ished! He hath saved us! On - ly trust to what He saith;
All the cloud of black transgression, He Him - self hath blot-ted out;

Oh re - turn, for His own life-blood Paid the ran-som, made us free
He hath done it! come and bless Him, Spend in praise your ransomed breath
He hath done it! come and bless Him, Swell the grand thanksgiving shout

ff *pp*

Ev-er-more and ev - er-more; Ev-er-more and ev-er-more.
Ev-er-more and ev - er-more; Ev-er-more and ev-er-more.
Ev-er-more and ev - er-more; Ev-er-more and ev-er-more.

HORATIUS BONAR.

GEO. C. HUGG.

1. I was a wand'ring sheep, I did not love the fold,
2. The Shep-herd sought his sheep, The Fa-ther sought his child;
3. Je-sus my Shepherd is; 'Twas He that loved my soul,
4. No more a wand'ring sheep, I love to be con-trolled,

I did not love my Shepherd's voice, I would not be con-trolled:
He fol-lowed me o'er vale and hill, O'er des-erts waste and wild:
'Twas He that washed me in His blood, 'Twas He that made me whole:
I love my ten-der Shepherd's voice, I love the peace-ful fold:

I was a way-ward child, I did not love my home,
He found me nigh to death, Famished, and faint, and lone;
'Twas He that sought the lost, That found the wan-d'ring sheep,
No more a way-ward child, I seek no more to roam;

I did not love my Fa-ther's voice, I loved a-far to roam.
He bound me with the bands of love, He saved the wand'ring one.
'Twas He that brought me to the fold, 'Tis He that still doth keep.
I love my heav'nly Fa-ther's voice, I love, I love His home!

SEND OUT THE LIFE-BOAT.

L. W. Smith.   F. A. Blackmer.

1. There are wrecks a - long the shore, Go-ing down on ev-'ry side, 'Mid the
2. Anxious friends are waiting lone, For an ab-sent, way ward child, Hearing
3. "May some an - gel from a - bove, Guard my child from ev'ry ill ; God of
4. Christian ! lis - ten to the voice, To the res - cue, haste a-way ! Let the

crashing breaker's roar, And the surging, foaming tide, Faintly o-ver rock and
not the saddened moan, Thro' the darkness, strange and wild, Hear the mother's earnest
mer-cy ! God of love, May it be Thy blessed will, Now to save my darl-ing
sons of God re-joice At the vic'try gained to-day, Christian! heed thy Saviour's

reef Comes the ag - o - niz-ing cry, "Send, oh ! send us quick relief ! Ere we
plea, Go-ing up to heav'n and God, "Send oh ! send Thy help to me ! Let me
boy ! Send some strong and loving hand, Ere the waves of sin destroy, That shall
call, Glad-ly His sweet will o - bey ; Point the dying, sink-ing soul, To the

CHORUS.

per - ish, ere we die."
lean up - on Thy rod."
bring him safe to land."
Life, the Truth, the way.
Send out the life - boat, Throw out the line !

Je - sus is call - ing in mer - cy divine; Thousands of time wrecks are

sink - ing in sin, Speed thro' the tem-pest and gath - er them in.

SWEETLY SING.

CENNICK.   PLEYEE.

1. Children of the heav'nly King! As ye jour-ney sweet-ly sing;
2. We are trav'-ling home to God, In the way the fa-thers trod;
3. Shout, ye lit-tle flock and blest! You on Je-sus' throne shall rest;
4. Fear not, brethern! joy-ful stand On the bor-ders of your land;
5. Lord! o - bedi-ent-ly we go, Glad-ly leav-ing all be-low;

Sing your Sa - viour's worthy praise, Glorious in His works and ways.
They are hap-py now, and we Soon their hap-pi-ness shall see.
There, your seat is now prepared,— There's your kingdom and re-ward.
Je - sus Christ, your Father's Son, Bids you un-dis-mayed go on.
On-ly Thou our Lead-er be, And we still will fol-low Thee.

LAND OF PROMISE.

Geo. C. Hugg.

Geo. C. Hugg.

1. There is a land, from sorrow free! 'Tis just a - cross the "Jas-per sea,"
2. There Zi - on stands se-rene - ly fair, With jeweled wall of diamonds square,
3. Oh joy of joys, supremely blest! Where pillowed on my Saviour's breast,

The "Tree of life" in heal-ing stands, In that im - mor - tal land.
With streets of Gold, and gates of pearl, I long to en - ter there.
I live with Him, He dwells with me, Thro' all e - ter - ni - ty.

CHORUS.

Oh land of light, oh fadeless bloom! Oh life be-yond the dis - mal

tomb! Oh Zi - on, cit - y fair and grand! God grant me peace in thee!

HOLY, HOLY!

Reg. Heber.   J. B. Dykes.

1. Ho - ly, ho - ly, ho - ly! Lord God Al - might - y!
2. Ho - ly, ho - ly, ho - ly! all the saints a - dore Thee,
3. Ho - ly, ho - ly, ho - ly! though the darkness hide Thee,
4. Ho - ly, ho - ly, ho - ly! Lord God Al - might - y!

Ear - ly in the morn - ing our song shall rise to Thee;
Cast - ing down their gold-en crowns a - round the glass - y sea;
Though the eye of sin - ful man Thy glo - ry may not see;
All Thy works shall praise Thy name, in earth and sky and sea;

Ho - ly, ho - ly, ho - ly, mer - ci - ful and might - y,
Cher - u - bim and ser - a - phim fall - ing down be - fore Thee,
On - ly Thou art ho - ly; there is none be - side Thee,
Ho - ly, ho - ly, ho - ly! mer - ci - ful and might - y,

God in three per - sons, bless - ed Trin - i - ty!
Which wert and art and ev - er - more shall be.
Per - fect in pow'r, in love and pur - i - ty.
God in three per - sons, bless - ed Trin - i - ty!

LIVING WATER.

GEO. C. HUGG.   GEO. C. HUGG.

Joyously.

1. O come to the liv - ing stream, The Wa - ter of Life is free;
2. Call ye on the Lord to -' day, He's pass-ing a - long the way,
3. Thy cry He will an - swer now, If low at His feet ye bow;

No price need ye pay, Sal - va - tion to - day Is flowing a-bund-ant - ly.
So ten-der, and near, "Thy call He will hear," Awake sinner, rise and pray!
O sin-ner re-lent! For Je - sus was sent To ransom thee with His blood.

CHORUS.

"The Spir-it and Bride say, Come!" And drink of the heal - ing stream,

Life-giv-ing and free, Tis flowing for thee ; O drink ye, and live al - way.

HORATIUS BONAR.　　　　　　　　　　　RICHARD REDHEAD.

1. Not to an-gels hath been granted The dear flock of God to keep;
2. Not to an-gels are com-mit-ted The green pas-tures of the flock;
3. They are wise, and strong, and ho-ly, On their er-rands will they speed,
4. Not to an-gels, but to sin-ners Is the great com-mis-sion giv'n,

Not to them hath the Chief Shepherd Ev-er spo-ken, "Feed my sheep;"
Not to them the qui-et wa-ters, Nor the shad-ow of the rock.
But they may not teach a par-don Which they do not, can-not need;
Now to point their fel-low wand'rers To the o-pen gate of heav'n;

Not to an-gels, by the Mas-ter, "Feed my lambs" was ev-er said;
Not to an-gel love be-long-eth The sweet balm for sor-rows deep;
They are care-ful, ten-der lov-ing, As God's min-is-ter-ing host;
And to us, who once have wondered, It is giv'n to show the road,

Not by an-gels are they gathered, Are they tend-ed, are they fed.
For the an-gels nev-er sor-row, And the an-gels nev-er weep.
But they can-not preach a gos-pel Which is on-ly for the lost.
To the fold of rest and safe-ty, To the bless-ed home of God.

HOMEWARD BOUND.

Horatius Bonar.   Geo. C. Hugg.

1. This is not my place of rest-ing, Mine's a cit - y yet to come;
2. In it all is light and glo - ry, O'er it shines a nightless day;
3. There the Lamb, our Shepherd, leads us, By the streams of life a - long;
4. Soon we pass this des-ert drea-ry, Soon we bid fare-well to pain;

Onward to it I am hasting, On to my e - ter-nal home.
Ev-'ry trace of sin's sad sto - ry, All the curse has passed a - way.
On the fresh-est pas-tures feeds us, Turns our sigh-ing in - to song.
Nev-er more be sad and wea-ry, Nev-er more to sin a - gain.

Chorus.

Homeward bound! homeward bound! Praise the Lord I'm homeward bound!
Homeward bound! homeward bound!

Mine is yon ce - les-tial cit - y, Praise the Lord I'm homeward bound.

GEO. C. HUGG.　　　　　　　　　　　　　　　GEO. C. HUGG.

Feelingly.

1. Oh what a prom-ise God has giv'n, To sin-ful mor-tals here;
2. The heart by pain and anguish riv'n, Yearns for one ray of cheer;
3. On Zi-on's heights, arrayed in white, Re-deem-ed loved ones stand;

A hope, a joy un-speak-a-ble, To wipe the fall-ing tear.
Grieve not, O soul, for God shall wipe A-way the fall-ing tear.
No mourn-ful day, nor tear-ful night, In E-den's hap-py land.

CHORUS.

For God shall wipe all tears a-way, All tears a-way, all tears a-way, For

God shall wipe all tears a-way, And turn our darkness in-to day...........

THE MORNING.

Geo. C. Hugg.

Geo. C. Hugg.

Not too fast.

1. When we rise to greet the Mas-ter in the morn-ing, In the
2. We shall see the Saints and Prophets in the morn-ing, In the
3. All who put their trust in Je-sus, in the morn-ing, In the

morn-ing, in the morn-ing; What a meet-ing of the faithful in the
morn-ing, in the morn-ing; Standing with the saved in Je-sus in the
morn-ing, in the morn-ing; Shall be gathered as His jew-els in the

morn - ing; When the res-ur-rec-tion dawn ap-pears.
morn - ing; When the res-ur-rec-tion dawn ap-pears.
morn - ing; To a-bide with Him for ev-er-more.

CHORUS.

In the morn - - ing, in the morn - - ing, When the
In the morn of morns so bright, in the morn of morns so bright,

sun has lost its light, And the stars no lon - ger bright; In the
In the

morn - - ing, in the morn - - ing, When the
morn of morns so bright, in the morn of morns so bright,

faithful shall their Saviour see, In the morn - - ing, in the
In the morn of morns so bright, in the

morn - - ing; We shall wake to reign with Je - sus in the
morn of morns so bright,

morn - - ing, Bless - ed morn - ing of E - ter - ni - ty.

ASK, SEEK, KNOCK!

Rev. W. T. Dale.   D. E. Dortch.

TRIO.

1. Ask, for the Fa-ther is read-y to hear, Je-sus is wait-ing your
2. Seek, while this pardon may freely be found, Ere the brief day of His
3. Knock, for the Saviour will o-pen the door, Kind-ly He's wait-ing to

pray'r to re-ceive; Ask-ing in faith, you have noth-ing to fear,
mer-cy is past, While His rich gra-ces so ful-ly a-bound,
wel-come you in; Come, ere the sea-son of grace shall be o'er,

Come, and the words of His prom-ise be-lieve.
And the free of-fer of mer-cy shall last.   } Ask, seek,
Ere you're re-ject-ed and die in your sin.

knock, His grace is a-bund-ant and free;

Ask, seek, knock, A bless-ing is wait-ing for thee.

By permission from " Grace and Glory."

S. BARING-GOULD.   A. S. SULLIVAN.

1. Onward, Christian sol - diers! marching as to war; With the cross of
2. Like a might-y   ar - my moves the Church of God, Brothers, we are
3. Crowns and thrones may per-ish ; kingdoms rise and wane ; But the Church of
4. Onward, then, ye peo - ple ; join our hap-py throng, Blend with ours your

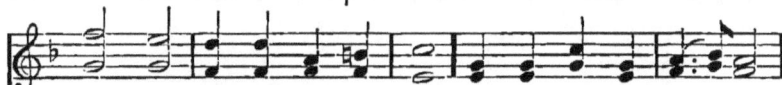

Je - sus go - ing on be - fore. Christ, the roy - al Mas - ter,
tread - ing where the saints have trod. We are not di - vi - ded,
Je - sus con - stant will re - main. Gates of hell can nev - er
voi - ces in the tri - umph song. Glor - y, laud and hon - or

leads a-gainst the foe, Forward in - to bat - tle see, his ban-ners go.
all one bod - y we, One in hope and doc - trine: one in char - i - ty.
'gainst that Church prevail, We have Christ's own promise, and that can-not fail
un - to Christ the King' This thro' countless a - ges men and an - gels sing.

CHORUS.

On - ward, Chris - tian sol - diers! March-ing as to war;

With the cross of Je - sus go - ing on be - fore.

ANYWHERE WITH JESUS.

Arr. by GEO. C. HUGG.

GEO. C. HUGG.

1. An - y - where with Je - sus, says the chris - tian heart,
2. An - y - where with Je - sus, will I glad - ly go,
3. An - y - where with Je - sus, till the con - flict's past,

An - y - where with Je - sus, so we do not part;
An - y - where with Je - sus, in this vale be - low,
An - y - where with Je - sus, faith - ful to the last,

An - y - where with Je - sus, there's no cause for fears;
An - y - where with Je - sus, His dear cross to bear;
Then with Saints in glo - ry sweet - ly will we sing,

CHORUS.

An - y-where with Jesus, in this vale of tears. } Anywhere with Je-sus,
An - y-where with Jesus, all His glo - ries share. }
Safe at home with Jesus, neath His shelt'ring wing. } Safe at home with Jesus,

an - y - where with Je - sus, An - y - where with Je - sus will I
safe at home with Je - sus, Safe at home with Je - sus with the

glad - ly go, An - y-where with Jesus, He will bear me thro'.
blood-washed band ! Safe at home with Jesus in the glo - ry - land !

TO-DAY.

S. F. SMITH.

GEO. C. HUGG.

1. To - day the Sa - viour calls; Ye wan - drers come;
2. To - day the Sa - viour calls; Oh hear Him now;
3. To - day the Sa - viour calls; For ref - uge fly;
4. The Spir - it calls to - day; Yield to His pow'r;

O ye be - night-ed souls ! Why long - er roam?
With - in these sa - cred walls, To Je - sus bow.
The storms of jus - tice fall; And death is nigh.
Oh ! grieve Him not a - way; 'Tis mer - cy's hour.

DOST THOU SEE THEM?

John M. Neale.   J. B. Dykes.

1. Chris-tian, dost thou see them, On the ho-ly ground,
2. Chris-tian, dost thou feel them, How they work with - in,
3. Chris-tian, dost thou hear them, How they speak thee fair?
4. Well I know thy trou-ble, O my serv-ant true;

How the pow'rs of e - vil Rage thy steps a - round?
Striv-ing, tempt-ing lur - ing, Goad-ing on to sin?
"Al - ways fast and vig - il? Al - ways watch and pray'r?"
Thou art ver - y wea - ry,— I was wea - ry too;

Chris - tian up and smite them, Count - ing gain but loss:
Chris - tian nev - er trem - ble; Nev - er yield to fear.
Chris - tian an - swer bold - ly; "While I breathe, I pray:"
But that toil shall make thee, Some-day all my own;

Smite them by the mer - it Of the ho - ly Cross.
Smite them by the vir - tue Of un - ceas - ing pray'r.
Peace shall fol - low bat - tle, Night shall end in day.
And the end of sor - row Shall be near my throne.

HUMILITY.

J. D. CARLYLE.   J. B. DYKES.

1. Lord, when we bend be-fore Thy throne, And our con-fes-sions pour;
2. When we dis-close our wants in pray'r, May we our wills re-sign;

Teach us to feel the sins we own, And hate what we de - plore;
And not a thought our bos-om share, Which is not whol-ly Thine;

Our bro-ken spir-it pity-ing see; True pen-i-tence im-part;
Let faith each meek pe-ti-tion fill, And waft it to the skies;

Then let a kind-ling glance from Thee Bear hope on ev-'ry heart.
And teach our hearts 'tis good-ness still, That grants it, or de-nies.

IS IT NOTHING TO ME?

E. R. LATTA.   H. S. PERKINS, by per.

SOLO.

1. Is it noth-ing to me That the dear Son of God, For the
2. Is it noth-ing to me That He suf-fered our pain? That to
3. Is it noth-ing to me That they laugh'd Him to scorn? That His
4. Is it noth-ing to me That my Lord was de-scried? On the
5. It is something to me! It is some-thing to you! Let us

sins of the world, Shed His in - no - cent blood? For the sins of the
bring us to God On the Cross He was slain? That to bring us to
hands and His feet Were so cru - el - ly torn? That His hands and His
dread Ro - man cross, That He suf-fered and died? On the dread Ro - man
give Him our hearts, And His blest bid-ding do! Let us give Him our

dim. e rit.   CHORUS.

world, Shed His in - no - cent blood? ⎫
God On the Cross He was slain? ⎪
feet Were so cru - el - ly torn? ⎬ Yes,'tis something to me, Yes 'tis
cross, That He suf - fered and died? ⎪
hearts, And His blest bid-ding do! ⎭

something to me: That our Lord for the world Shed His in - no-cent blood.

F. R. HAVERGAL.

F. R. HAVERGAL.

1. Golden harps are sounding, An-gel voic-es ring, Pearly gates are o-pened,
2. He who came to save us, He who bled and died, Now is crowned with gladness
3. Pray-ing for His chil-dren In that blessed place, Calling them to glo-ry,

O-pened for the King. Christ, the King of Glory, Je - sus, King of love,
At his Father's side. Nev-er more to suf - fer, Nev-er more to die,
Sending them His grace ; His bright home preparing, Lit-tle ones, for you ;

CHORUS.

Is gone up in triumph To His throne a - bove.
Je-sus, King of Glo-ry, Is gone up on high. } All His work is end - ed,
Je-sus ev - er liv - eth, Ev - er lov -eth too.

Joy-ful-ly we sing ; Je-sus hath as-cend-ed ! Glo-ry to our King !

TOILING HOMEWARD.

E. W. CHAPMAN.

FRANK M. DAVIS.

Trustingly.

1. Man-y foes thy path be-set, Watch a lit-tle lon-ger,
2. O be-liev-er in the Lord, Hope a lit-tle lon-ger,
3. An-gels hold a-jar the door, March a lit-tle lon-ger,
4. Be thou faith-ful un-to death, Firm a lit-tle lon-ger,

By the love of God close-kept, Let thy faith grow stron-ger;
Cour-age now, thy head lift up, And thro' Christ grow stron-ger;
O'er the threshold thou wilt pass With re-li-ance stron-ger;
In the foot-steps of the Lord Walk a lit-tle lon-ger;

Thro' His pow'r and grace stand fast, Vanquished ev-'ry foe at last,
In thy Sa-viour rest each hour, Safe thy soul in this strong tow'r,
Just with-in the gold-en gate, Saints and an-gels for thee wait,
Ends thy path in bloom-ing spring, He'll thee thro' the gate-way bring.

All thy sins be-hind thee cast, Toil a lit-tle lon-ger.
Gain-ing there a price-less dow'r, Trust a lit-tle lon-ger.
Joy-ing in thy blest es-tate, March a lit-tle lon-ger.
Then the new, new song to sing, Sing for-ev-er yon-der.

Thomas J. Potter.

Haydn.

1. Brightly gleams our banner, Pointing to the sky, Waving wand'rers onward
2. Je-sus, Lord and Mas-ter, At Thy sa-cred feet, Here with hearts rejoicing
3. All our days di-rect us In the way we go; Lead us on vic-to-rious

To their home on high, Journey o'er the des-ert Glad-ly thus we pray,
See Thy children meet; Often have we left Thee, Oft-en gone a - stray;
O - ver ev - 'ry foe: Bid Thine angels shield us, When the storm clouds low'r;

CHORUS.

And with hearts united, Take our heav'nward way.
Keep us, Mighty Saviour, In the narrow way. } Brightly gleams our banner
Pardon thou and save us, In the last dread hour.

Pointing to the sky, Waving wand'rers onward To their home on high.

GLORY TO GOD.

Thomas MacKellar.   Geo. C. Hugg.

Maestoso.

1. Glo - ry to God! Glo - ry to God! Glo - ry to God
2. Glo - ry to God! Glo - ry to God! Glo - ry to God
3. Glo - ry to God! Glo - ry to God! Glo - ry to God
4. Glo - ry to God! Glo - ry to God! Glo - ry to God
5. Glo - ry to God! Glo - ry to God! Glo - ry to God

Allegro.

in the high - - est! The day of all
in the high - - est! Let heav - en re -
in the high - - est! Let earth, with its
in the high - - est! His good - will and
in the high - - est! The boun - ti - ful

days A - wak - ens our praise,— The
sound To its ut - ter - most bound With
hills, Its val - leys and rills, Re -
peace To men will not cease: The
Lord,— The Fath - er, the Word, The

thrice - bless - ed morn When Je - sus was born,— The
an - thems of praise Both now and al - ways, While
ech - o His praise Both now and al - ways, While
church lifts her voice While an - gels re - joice, And
Spir - it,— whose praise Both now and al - ways On

name that   the   church glo - ri - fi - eth:
ser - aph   to   ser - aph re - pli - eth,
moun - tain to   moun - tain - top cri - eth,
her song   with the   seraph - im's vi - eth:
the wings   of   in - fin - ity fli - eth:

Glo - ry   to   God! Glo - ry   to   God!

Glo - ry   to   God   in   the   high - est!

Glo - ry   to   God   in   the   high - est!

PARADISE.

F. W. FABER.   H. HEMY.

1. O Par - a - dise, O Par - a - dise, Who doth not crave for rest?
2. O Par - a - dise, O Par - a - dise, The world is grow-ing old.
3. O Par - a - dise, O Par - a - dise, 'Tis wea - ry wait-ing here;
4. O Par - a - dise, O Par - a - dise, I want to sin no more,
5. O Par - a - dise, O Par - a - dise, I great - ly want to see
6. Lord Je - sus, King of Par - a - dise, O keep me in Thy love,

Who would not seek the hap-py land Where they that loved are blest?
Who would not be at rest and free Where love is nev - er cold?
I long to be where Je - sus is, To feel, to see Him near;
I want to be as pure on earth As on Thy spot - less shore;
The spec-ial place, my dear-est Lord, In love pre - pares for me:
And guide me to that hap-py land Of per - fect rest a - bove,

CHORUS.

Where loy - al hearts and true Stand ev - er in the light,

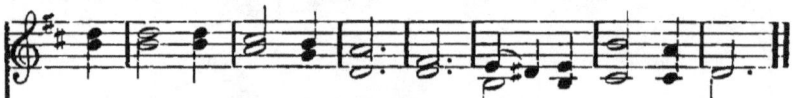

All rap-ture through and through, In God's most ho - ly sight.

C. WORDSWORTH.   H. HEMY.

1. O Day   of rest and glad-ness, O   day   of joy and light,
2. On thee, at the cre - a - tion, The light first had its birth,
3. Thou art a   cool-ing foun-tain, In life's dry drear-y sand:
4. To - day on wea - ry na - tions The heav'n-ly Man - na falls,
5. New gra - ces ev - er gain-ing From this our day of rest,

O balm of care and sad - ness, Most beau-ti - ful, most bright;
On thee for our sal - va - tion Christ rose from depths of earth;
From thee, like Pis - gah's moun-tain, We view our prom-ised land;
To ho - ly con - vo - ca - tions The sil - ver trum-pet calls,
We reach the Rest re - main - ing To spir-its of the blest;

On thee the high and low - ly   Be - fore the eter - nal Throne,
On thee our Lord vic - to - rious The Spir - it sent from heav'n;
A   day of sweet re - flec - tion, A day of ho - ly love,
Where Gos-pel-light is glow-ing, With pure and ra - diant beams,
To Ho - ly Ghost be prais - es, To Fa - ther and to Son;

Sing Ho - ly, Ho - ly, Ho - ly, To the great Three in One.
And thus on thee most glo - rious A   trip - le light was giv'n.
A   day of res - ur - rec - tion From earth to things a - bove.
And liv - ing wa - ter flow - ing With soul re - fresh-ing streams.
The Church her voice up - rais - es To Thee, blest Three in One.

CITY OF GOD.

Selected.

H. HEMY.

1. Dai - ly, dai - ly sing the praises Of the Cit - y God hath made.
2. All the streets of that dear Cit - y Are of bright and burnished gold;
3. In the midst of that dear Cit - y Christ is reign - ing on His seat,
4. From the throne a riv - er is - sues, Clear as crys - tal, pass - ing bright,
5. There the meadows green and dewy Shine with lil - ies wondrous fair;
6. There the wind is sweetly fragrant, And is la - den with the song,

In the beauteous fields of E - den Its foun - da - tion-stones are laid.
It is matchless in its beau - ty, And its treasures are un - told.
And the an - gels swing their censers In a ring a - bout His feet.
And it tra - ver - ses the Cit - y Like a sud - den beam of light.
Thousand, thousand are the col - ors Of the wav - ing flow - ers there.
Of the Ser - aphs, and the El - ders, And the great re - deem - ing throng.

CHORUS.

O that I had wings of an - gels Here to spread and heav'nward fly,

I would seek the gates of Zi - on, Far be - yond the star - ry sky.

J. H. NEWMAN.   J. B. DYKES.

1. Lead, kindly Light! amid the encircling gloom,   Lead Thou me   on;
2.   I was not ev - er thus, nor prayed that Thou   Shouldst lead me on;
3. So long Thy power hast blest me, sure it still   Will lead me   on

The night is dark, and I am far from   home ;   Lead Thou me   on ;
I loved to choose and see my path ; but now   Lead Thou me   on ;
O'er moor and fen, o'er crag and torrent, till   The night is gone ;

Keep Thou my   feet ;   I   do not   ask   to   see
I   loved the   gar - ish day, and, spite of   fears,
And with the   morn those an - gel fa - ces   smile

The   dis - tant   scene ; one step e - nough   for   me.
Pride ruled my   will. Re - mem - ber   not   past years.
Which I   have   loved long since, and lost   a   while !

G. B. LISSANT.
G. B. LISSANT.

1. We are sol-diers of the cross, Ours the old, old sto - ry;
2. Though a-round on ev - 'ry hand, Sat-an's hosts as - sail us,
3. As we raise our mar-tial song, Cour-age 'ne'er a - bat - ing,
4. See the heavn'ly mansions bright, Faithful hope a - dorn - ing;

Counting all our gain as loss But the gain for glo - ry.
We've a Cap-tain in com-mand Who will nev - er fail us,
An - gel bands, a ho - ly throng, On our steps are wait - ing.
Far be - hind us looms the night, But be - fore, the morn - ing:

In the path our fath-ers trod With their faith un - swerv - ing;
Fierce may rage the bat -tle strife, Noth-ing shall a - larm us;
Soon the jour-ney will be o'er, Passed each dark af - flic - tion;
On-ward, on-ward to the goal, Je - sus goes be - fore us;

Orgl Ped.

He - roes of the Church of God— So would we be serv - ing.
Press-ing to e - ter - nal life Not a shaft shall harm us.
Let us think how Je - sus bore Scourge and cru - ci - fix - ion.
Come, O come! each ran-somed soul Sound on high the cho - rus.

W. F. LLOYD. ENGLISH.

mf

1. Wait, my soul up - on the Lord, To His
2. If the sor - rows of thy case Seem pe -
3. Days of tri - al, days of grief, In suc -
4. Rock of a - ges! I'm se - cure, With Thy

gra - cious prom - ise flee, Lay - ing
cul - iar still to thee, God has
ces - sion thou mayest see; This is
prom - ise, full and free, Ev - er

hold up - on His word: "As thy days thy
prom - ised need - ful grace: "As thy days thy
still thy sweet re - lief: "As thy days thy
faith - ful, ev - er sure: "As thy days thy

strength shall be," "As thy days thy strength shall be."
strength shall be," "As thy days thy strength shall be."
strength shall be," "As thy days thy strength shall be."
strength shall be," "As thy days thy strength shall be."

G. W. BETHUNE.   ENGLISH.

With martial effect.

1. Come, let us sing of Je - sus, While hearts and accents blend;
2. We love to sing of Je - sus, Who wept our path a - long;
3. We love to sing of Je - sus, Who died our souls to save;
4. Then let us sing of Je - sus, While yet on earth we stay;

Come, let us sing of Je - sus, The sin - ner's on - ly Friend,
We love to sing of Je - sus, The temp - ted and the strong;
We love to sing of Je - sus, Tri - umphant o'er the grave;
And hope to sing of Je - sus Throughout e - ter - nal day;

His ho - ly soul re - joic - es, A - mid the choirs a - bove,
None who be - sought His heal - ing, He passed un-heed-ed by,
And in our hour of dan - ger, We'll trust His love a - lone,
For those who here con - fess Him, He will in heav'n con - fess.

To hear our tune-ful voic - es Ex - ult - ing in His love.
And still re - tains His feel - ing For us a - bove the sky.
Who once slept in a man - ger, And now sits on the throne.
And faith-ful hearts that bless Him He will for ev - er bless.

CHORUS.

Come, let us sing of Je-sus, His glo-rious name pro-claim,

Ped. marcato.

Come, let us sing of Je-sus, And laud His ho-ly name.

WELCOME DAY.

Isaac Watts.

G. B. Lissant.

1. Lo! what a glo-rious sight appears To our be-liev-ing eyes!
2. At-tend-ing an-gels shout for joy, And the bright ar-mies sing:
4. "His own soft hand shall wipe the tears From ev-'ry weep-ing eye,

The earth and sea are passed a-way, And the old roll-ing skies.
"Mor-tals, be-hold the sa-cred seat Of your de-scend-ing King.
And pains, and groans, and griefs and fears, And death it-self, shall die.

From the third heav'n, where God resides, That ho-ly, hap-py place,
"The God of glo-ry down to men Removes His blest a-bode—
How long, dear Sa-viour! oh, how long, Shall this bright hour de-lay?

The new Je-ru-sa-lem comes down, Adorned with shin-ing grace.
Men, the dear ob-jects of His grace, And He the lov-ing God.
Fly swift-er round, ye wheels of time, And bring the wel-come day.

∴ Music Typography, by W. H. Keyser & Co., Phila., Pa.

INDEX OF TITLES.

INDEX OF FIRST LINES.

————>※<————

www.ingramcontent.com/pod-product-compliance
Lightning Source LLC
Chambersburg PA
CBHW020546270326
41927CB00006B/744